Literacy, Play and Globalization

This book takes on current perspectives on children's relationships to literacy, media, childhood, markets and transtionalism in converging global worlds. It introduces the idea of multi-sited imaginaries to explain how children's media and literacy performances shape and are shaped by shared visions of communities that we collectively imagine, including play, media, gender, family, school, or cultural worlds. It draws upon elements of ethnographies of globalization, nexus analysis and performance theories to examine the convergences of such imaginaries across multiple sites: early childhood and elementary classrooms and communities in Puerto Rico and the Midwest United States. In this work we attempt to understand that the local moment of engagement within play, dramatic experiences, and literacies is not a given but is always emerging from and within the multiple localities children navigate and the histories, possibilities and challenges they bring to the creative moment.

Carmen Liliana Medina is an associate professor in Literacy Culture and Language Education at Indiana University. Her research focuses on literacy and biliteracy as social and critical practices. She has published in journals such as *Reading Research Quarterly*, *Language Arts*, *Theory into Practice* and the *Journal of Teacher Education*. She has a forthcoming co-edited volume with Dr. Mia Perry entitled *Methodologies of Embodiment* (Routledge Research Series).

Karen E. Wohlwend is an associate professor in Literacy, Culture, and Language Education in the School of Education at Indiana University. Her research critically examines young children's play with toys, popular media, and digital technologies. She has authored two books: *Literacy Playshop: Playing with New Literacies and Popular Media in the Early Childhood Classroom* and *Playing Their Way into Literacies: Reading, Writing and Belonging in the Early Childhood Classroom*.

Routledge Research in Education

For a full list of titles in this series, please visit www.routledge.com.

Literacy, Play and Globalization
Converging Imaginaries in Children's
Critical and Cultural Performances

**Carmen Liliana Medina
and Karen E. Wohlwend**

Routledge
Taylor & Francis Group
NEW YORK   LONDON

KH

First published 2014
by Routledge
711 Third Avenue, New York, NY 10017

and by Routledge
2 Park Square, Milton Park, Abingdon, Oxon OX14 4RN

*Routledge is an imprint of the Taylor & Francis Group,
an informa business*

Library of Congress Cataloging-in-Publication Data
Medina, Carmen Liliana.
    Literacy, play and globalization : converging imaginaries in children's
critical and cultural performances / Carmen Liliana Medina,
Karen E. Wohlwend.
        pages cm. — (Routledge research in education ; 115)
    Includes bibliographical references and index.
    1. Language arts (Early childhood)   2. Play.   3. Cultural
pluralism.   I. Wohlwend, Karen E.   II. Title.
    LB1139.5.L35M43 2014
    372.6—dc23
    2013044995

ISBN13: 978-0-415-63716-9 (hbk)
ISBN13: 978-0-203-08476-2 (ebk)

Typeset in Sabon
by IBT Global.

SUSTAINABLE   Certified Sourcing
FORESTRY   www.sfiprogram.org
INITIATIVE   SFI-01234
SFI label applies to the text stock

Printed and bound in the United States of America
by IBT Global.

12/17/15

Contents

PART III
Convergences in Collective Cultural Imaginaries

Figures

Tables

Foreword

Vivian Maria Vasquez

A friend once told me that the purpose of a foreword is to offer perspective and to tell the story of the book for which the foreword is written. For me, it was clear from the start that Carmen Medina and Karen Wohlwend's *Literacy, Play, and Globalization: Converging Imaginaries in Children's Critical and Cultural Performances* is a gift that has made its way to the field at a time of low morale when high-stakes testing and one-size-fits-all mandated curricular standards diminish the important work done by teachers across the nation. These trying times have resulted in some educators retreating from using words like *play* when talking about teaching and learning. While many have succumbed to the politics of a common core curriculum, in this book Carmen and Karen instead tell a story of venturing towards the boundaries, pushing and tugging at those boundaries to make visible new and important demonstrations of complex and sophisticated learning that is possible when topics and issues that matter in the lives of children are positioned as powerful curricular material, rather than predetermined prescriptive and standardized curricula. They push the boundaries by looking across research contexts as they unpack, embrace, and contest theories and methods in the study of globalization relative to children's ways of knowing and their engagement in literacy practices. They employ the use of contemporary global anthropology and ethnographic perspectives to do this work.

Through the years there have been numerous books on literacy, play, and young children, and an increasing number of books that focus on globalization. Each of these has informed the field in some way, but I am unaware of any text that pushes the boundaries by working at a literacy, play, and globalization nexus as it concerns young children. In their book, Carmen and Karen unpack and map out for their readers an intricately complex web of literacy and learning in and outside school, from a local–global, rural–urban, Spanish–English–multilingual, and multinational media perspective. They do this while taking on multiple sites; early childhood and elementary classrooms and communities in Puerto Rico and the Midwestern U.S. In Puerto Rico, for example, Carmen studied telenovela identity texts in relation to classroom literacy drama pedagogy in a third grade classroom. They did this in spite of the mandated national curricular basal reader, which is driven by federal policies of No Child Left Behind. In Iowa, Karen worked with a group of kindergarten children who performed and negotiated the meanings of "family" through the Disney Princess play among girls and boys with transnational connections to other countries. This multisited approach afforded them the space to create a framework to understand how global flows and the new imagined worlds of students become localized, making it possible for them to consider critically what it means to foreground the students' knowledge and engagement within these global flows, in relation to their lives, and unpack how these are made visible in their literacy work. This approach also afforded the use of a nexus analysis of classroom performative events, such as written and visual performances and media discussions.

What you get with *Literacy, Play, and Globalization* is a sophisticated and important text that creates new spaces for critical literacy educators and multiliteracies researchers to think about the complex world of globalization studies and literacy across research contexts. The book takes on transnationalism from different theoretical orientations while looking closely at children's relationships to media and childhood play. The book also puts on offer powerful discursive practices for talking about this work.

The book is divided into three parts. Part I primes the pump by providing an overview of the theories and research that creates a space for the possibility of framing a converging multimodal literacy curriculum that respects children's complex ways of living across time and space. Of particular significance is their conceptualization and development of multisited imaginaries. They use the term *imaginaries* to situate the children's complex worlds and ways of living within their lived cultural experiences, rather than in fantasy or in literature. They do this across both global and local sites. For example, they explore how children use drama, make-believe, and play to consume, explore, contest, disrupt, and reimagine global media identities and consumer identities.

Part II is what I believe to be the heart and soul of the book. In this part, we travel to Puerto Rico and to Iowa and become privy to the sights and sounds of life in and out of the classroom. The incidents and stories that unfold from these places stem from Carmen's and Karen's projects, as mentioned previously, which provide opportunities for reenvisioning the role of literacy, play, and dramatic experiences as cultural production.

The last part of the book, Part III, is a return to Carmen and Karen's cultural imaginaries model, where they take another look at cultural production at the intersections of globalization, literacy practices, and performance.

There are numerous takeaways from this book. But some of the most important takeaways are the spaces or ruptures created by Carmen and Karen for other researchers and teachers to collaborate and begin to imagine new spaces for extending the work presented in this book. To encourage this endeavor, at the end of the book they invite readers to question the limits of what can be made visible through elements of anthropology of globalization and literacy research practices by asking questions such as: What local/global worlds and networks do my students and I navigate in our/their everyday lives, and how do those worlds converge? Who gets privileged and who gets marginalized by global/local structures of power that circulate in my community, school, classroom, and literacy curriculum? Once these questions have been explored, it is possible then to ask further questions, such as: How do students navigate global or transnational landscapes as forms of curriculum inquiry as they share and interpret information through participation in real and imagined worlds?

In this courageous text, Carmen and Karen have laid the groundwork for us; it therefore behooves us to find our own ways of entering the spaces that they have so carefully created for us to begin our own explorations of literacy, play, and globalization.

Acknowledgments

Earlier partial versions of this research appeared as:

Medina, C. & Costa, M del R. (2013). Latino media and critical literacy pedagogies: Children's scripting Telenovelas discourses. *Journal of Language and Literacy Education, 9*(1). Copyright © by University of Georgia. http://jolle.coe.uga.edu.

Wohlwend, K. E. (2012). The boys who would be princesses: Playing with gender identity intertexts in Disney Princess transmedia. *Gender and Education, 24*(6), 593–610. Copyright © Taylor and Francis. www.tandfonline.com.

Wohlwend, K. E., & Medina, C. L. (2012). Media as nexus of practice: Remaking identities in What Not to Wear. *Discourse: Studies in the Cultural Politics of Education, 33*(4), 545–560. Copyright © Taylor and Francis. http://www.tandfonline.com/doi/abs/10.1080/01596306.2012.692961 [The full article is reprinted with permission in Appendix B.]

The research in this book was supported in part through grants from:

The National Council of Teachers of English Research Foundation Grant
Indiana University Summer Proffitt Grant
Indiana University Office of the Vice-Provost for Research Creative Grant

Part I

Literacy Research within Multisited Imaginaries and Converging Worlds

Collaborations emerge in unexpected but organic ways. This book is the product of numerous meetings and gatherings where we shared frameworks, ideas, data, and reflections on the work we do examining children's contemporary cultural practices and production in relation to sociocritical perspectives on literacy, play, dramatic experiences, and media. The book is a reflection of some of the transformative paths in our work that have intersected in the present moment. We bring to this work our past experiences that take sociocultural and critical perspectives on play, dramatic experiences, and texts, but we push the boundaries of our previous work to engage in the exercise of looking across research contexts as we unpack, embrace, and contest theories and methods in the study of globalization in relation to children's ways of knowing and their engagement in literacy practices. While later in this book we dedicate a section to methodologies and pedagogies that comprise multisited imaginaries in their design and notions of imagined worlds and communities, at this point we want to briefly describe what holds this book together and what emerged as a "convergence" in our collaborative work.

An element that is significant in our collaboration is our commitment to look beyond abstract, neutral, and disconnected understandings of how global flows and networks circulate in society. More specifically, in our particular research projects and in the process of sharing researcher stories and data sets, we have been able to understand and map how particular and how complex are children's participation in networks of global–local imagined worlds and how those worlds get reinterpreted and recontextualized by children within and across cultural locations. These engagements, recontextualizations, and reconstructions of worlds involve the politics embedded in participating, consuming, and producing within global/local sites that, according to Lewellen (2002), should be described as "unpredict-able interaction and creative adaption, and not top-down determinism" (back cover). For example, by examining the micro-political practices of children in relation to global discourses in colonial places, such as Puerto Rico, or in rural places, such as Iowa, we came to realize how global politics and ideologies, through children's participation across imagined worlds, become part of the contextual ways of knowing they enact in multiple sites of engagement or "habitats of meaning" (Hannerz, 1996), or the spaces people inhabit where they engage in shared meaning-making practices that are not limited to a geographical location (i.e., classroom, home, etc.). In order to share this complexity, we divided this book into three parts.

- Part I provides an overview of the theories and research that support our model of cultural imaginaries and provide the lenses for look-ing at imagined worlds across global–local sites. Chapters 1 and 2 introduce key issues and core concepts from theories of globalization, performance, and new literacies that are foundational to our model of collective imaginaries as cultural productions created through play and drama. In Chapter 2, we introduce our model of collective imagi-naries as the convergence of three spheres: ethnographies of globaliza-tion, nexus of practice, and performance. We draw on this diagram of converging spheres throughout the book, adding specific details for particular sites of engagement across the chapters.
- Part II provides data from classroom studies in Puerto Rico and Iowa, reanalyzed with these lenses. In Chapter 3, we examine how global imaginaries circulate in local sites through commercial media that flow into every inlet and outlet of communities and geographies, whether urban or rural, tropical or land-locked, populous or remote. In Chap-ter 4, Carmen shares her research on children's cultural production of imaginaries during a critical inquiry of telenovelas, popular Spanish melodramas, in collaboration with teachers in a third grade classroom in Puerto Rico. In Chapter 5, Karen examines children's cultural pro-duction of gendered imaginaries during Disney Princess play among transnational boys and girls in a kindergarten in Iowa. In Chapter 6, we look across our research to understand how adults' imaginaries of childhood and children's imaginaries of their own worlds converged and clashed, despite educators' best intentions.
- Part III returns to the model, looking at cultural production in the intersections of globalization, literacy practices, and performance. In Chapter 7, we take a step back to look at children's cultural produc-tion in the intersections of the three spheres in our model: multiple sites (e.g., classrooms, markets, media), expected cultural practices in those sites, and identity performances that improvise and rupture regularized and normative practices when sites converge. In Chap-ter 8, we explore the possibilities of imagination as a mediator of

globalization and convergence as a catalyst for change. In Chapter 9, we share how we are imagining otherwise with preservice and in-service teachers as we unpack the implications of this approach for teacher education.

In Part I, we lay the foundation for our reimagining of the relationships of play, literacy, globalization, and childhood. Chapter 1 identifies key understandings from research on ethnographies of globalization, nexus of practice, and performance. In Chapter 2, we explain our model of cultural production within converging, collective imaginaries.

1 Global Networks, Cultural Production, and Literacy Practices

> To understand globalization, we must study it at the level of real people who imagine new lives, make plans, form networks, assume identities and socialize their children
>
> —*The Anthropology of Globalization* (Lewellen, 2002, p. 26)

Current perspectives on transnationalism, media engagement, and the politics of childhood and global markets help us understand how children engage and interpret their relationships in converging global worlds and how they accommodate and/or resist these social dynamics in their local contexts. Under these social conditions, children live multiliterate lives as they move as consumers and producers of knowledge across real and imagined spaces, across worlds and communities, and in textual diasporas grounded in traveling texts that flow through media, digital spaces, and the consumption structures of global markets. In social sciences and cultural studies research, according to Lipitz (2005), "we need to learn from people and cultures that have been forced to make themselves as mobile, flexible, and fluid as transnational capital, yet still capable of drawing upon separate histories, principles, and values" (Lipitz, cited in Maira & Soep, 2005, p. xix). The rationale for this statement comes from the need to understand contemporary dynamics in cultural production and economic development in relation to converging social phenomena, such as people's access to global media and technology, diasporic moves across nations, and access to and imposition of multinational economic markets. Youth's and children's engagement with(in) these global dynamics play a critical role in society (Luke, 2004; Luke, Iyer & Doherty, 2010). Children's social imaginations in contemporary times are embedded in fluid but also disjointed and fragmented cultural practices with multimodal textual resources that are not static or tethered to one particular place yet carry attached histories and ideologies that become traces of multiple localities. Therefore, reading, writing, and cultural production happen at the intersection of participation in complex worlds and discourses that cannot be ignored when visualizing literacy pedagogies that matter to/for children.

Working in the complex and contradictory space within and against globalization (Bauman, 1998; Appadurai, 1996 & 2006), in this book we share our experiences in the study of globalization landscapes and discourses in relation to local communities, classroom literacy pedagogies, and childhood. We specifically examine children's interpretive dynamics and cultural production as they enact their knowledge and experiences in their engagement with global multinational media networks and markets, transnationalism and flows of knowledge across multiple *habitats of meaning* (Hannerz, 1996), or the spaces people inhabit to engage in cultural practices that are not necessarily related to one material geographical location. The purpose of our collaborative work is to make sense of how these experiences are relocated in complicated ways in classrooms and communities. In our work as literacy researchers, we are committed to exploring ways of doing research that disrupt the perceived boundaries between global–local and in–out of school and engage in an analysis of unfixed, contested, and localized pedagogies that allow us to map and unpack the complex dynamics of how children live and negotiate converging worlds. In our engagement with global networks and discourses embedded in these landscapes, we work with children in analytical processes, narrative construction, and play/dramatic experiences.

These dense sites of production provide ways of mapping children's access and engagement with a wide range of local and global networks and cultural practices. In these translocal spaces, the boundaries of literacy curriculum design are pushed beyond bounded notions of local and national discourses or standards and fixed expectations. Instead, these sites of convergence facilitate a new form of critical engagement that moves across *imagined communities* (Anderson, 1983) and *imagined worlds* (Appadurai, 1996). These moves involve pedagogical practices that put at the forefront children's *intercultural capital* (Luke, 2004), knowledge gathered by living between local and global worlds and by developing the "capacity to engage in acts of knowledge, power and exchange across time/space divides and social geographies, across diverse communities, populations and epistemic stances" (p. 1429).

Using the students' interests and self-selected choices to work (with)in and across global, local, and transnational networks as a framework for curriculum design, in this book we focus on classroom engagements where worlds converge, and interpret those engagements as forms of *scripting* (Appadurai, 1996; Soep, 2005), where local identity practices, narratives, and discourses interact with complex global economies, landscapes, and ideologies. Furthermore, in order to create a rich map of children's converging worlds in relation to pedagogy, we extend our work using contemporary global anthropology and ethnographic perspectives on the study of multisited imaginaries—particularly media spectacles as "sites" for the creation of contested imagined worlds—to interpret and understand the relationship among multinational global networks and its "presence" in the nexus of everyday practices (Scollon 2001) that creates and sustains an imagined local community.

Our emphasis is on moves that happen through children's engagement with transnational media, in relation to other complex translocal negotiations, and their participation in *collective imaginaries* constructed through shared practices, identity performances, and discourses. We use the term *imaginaries* to situate these worlds in children's lived cultural experiences, rather than in fantasy or literature. We want to share our experiences and ways of looking at children's literacy practices, hoping to provide a framework that disrupts the artificial distinctions imposed by in-/out-of-school, local–global, face-to-face–digital, or geopolitical boundaries and open up the possibility of framing a converging multimodal literacy curriculum that responds to children's complex ways of living.

The book is framed by the following questions:

- How do children mediate and participate within and across cultural imaginaries as nexus of practice (Scollon, 2001) that are made available to them in their everyday lives in their local communities and across other communities?
- How and what is made visible through a performance lens that foregrounds multiplicity of discourses and identities as well as emergence and convergence in and across imagined communities and worlds?
- How do playful and dramatic literacy pedagogies help children critically and collectively negotiate, enact, disrupt, and improvised new scripts and identities in relation to complex global ecologies?
- How do these practices help us reconceptualize children's agency and envision a critical literacy pedagogy as *scripting practices* in classrooms, foregrounding the role of the imagination as a social practice?

CONVERGING RESEARCH SPACES THROUGH COLLABORATIONS: MAPPING COMPLEX IMAGINED WORLDS, CULTURAL PRACTICES, AND EMERGING IDENTITIES

To explore the questions that frame this book, we needed to foreground the power and political discourses that circulate in local, national, and global spaces as part of children's nexus of practice to see how these flows become forms of participation in imagined worlds through embodied engagement in activities negotiating global discourses and artifacts. While mobility, flows, and translocalities seem to describe important conditions in our contemporary society, this does not means that dominant ideologies are dispersed without consequences (Bauman, 2007; Castells, 1999; Mazarella, 2004; Ong, 1999; Santos, 2006, 2007; Appadurai, 2006). Sharing a reflective researcher space, we looked across studies in Puerto Rico and Iowa to see how play, dramatic experiences, and literacies interact with global media and its dominant gender discourses and other social discourses that permeate children's lives across contexts or how the global politics of economic struggles are made visible in relation to local struggles in children's relocations of media power. We believe this kind of critical reflection across research contexts could provide multiliteracies researchers and critical literacy educators with windows into contemporary culture, resulting in a broader conceptual framework to understand literacy, diversity, and children's critical engagement with texts.

Our intentions are not to create a deterministic, fixed, or top-down view of globalization. Each context we share is unique and the students' engagements more so. Similar to researchers who work in anthropologies of globalization, we look across classroom projects and the multiple communities children navigate to share dynamics of globalization that are unpredictable, creative, always emerging, political, constitutive of, and constituted by children's agentic and identity work in situated contexts and moments in time. It is our hope that readers who engage with our work can find connections to their own views into classrooms and communities. Even more than connecting with our work, we are hoping that readers search for the gaps as it is impossible to get a complete picture of the fragmented and fragmenting phenomena of globalization (Bauman, 2007). In other words, we encourage readers to question the limits of what we can make visible through elements of anthropology of globalization and literacy research practices and ask questions such as:

- What local–global worlds and networks do my students and I navigate in our/their everyday lives and how do those worlds converge?
- What are the situated local–global dynamics in my community (through migratory movements, media, and/or multinational global market domination)? What's my relationship with these social dynamics? What are the histories and politics behind these dynamics? Who gets privileged and who gets marginalized by global–local structures of power that circulate in my community, school, classroom, and literacy curriculum?

Once these questions have been explored, it is possible then to ask further questions:

- What are the imagined communities and worlds of practice my students become part of beyond the classroom or their immediate physical/local spaces?
- How do students navigate global or transnational landscapes as forms of curriculum inquiry as they share and interpret information through participation in real and imagined worlds?
- What dominant politics and power ideologies are embedded or how are children marginalized in participating in these communities?
- How can we reinvent literacy pedagogies that productively engage children in deconstructing and splintering those dynamics into forms of alter-global discourses (Bauman, 1998)?

- How can productive playful pedagogies make use of such ruptures and invent new forms of doing critical literacy that move from strategies to strategizing or *scripting practices*?

These questions could help readers to relocate the meanings and interpretations we share in this book. The key element in this process is to understand that the global–local is not a location but a networked multisited interaction that is complex and never neutral or universal. What is local for some becomes global for others with consequences that are unique to each context. As Mazarella (2004) suggests, what becomes worth studying through critical inquiries of globalization are the "nodes of mediation" or what we call "convergences" that allow us to see "where value is often produced and contested, more or less self-consciously, in the name of culture" (p. 345). It is this complexity and uniqueness, foregrounding the notion of convergences, that we want to highlight by looking across our research spaces.

We situate our book in perspectives on literacy as social practice (Gee, 1996; Street, 1995; Lewis, 2001; Vasquez, 2004) and media as participatory culture (Jenkins, 2006) that argue media, like literacies, permeate multiple disciplines and circulate as cultural practices. We foreground our analysis on literacy and media, two dominant childhood imaginaries where young children engage in cultural production regularly through their everyday routines and ordinary traversals across homes, classrooms, communities, and markets. Engagement in *mediascapes*—"the distribution of electronic capabilities to produce and disseminate information" (Appadurai, 1996, p. 35)—emerged as a key aspect in children's lives both in Puerto Rico and Iowa. Such engagements played out in unique localized ways, but in both cases were constituted in relation to other global networks or scapes such as immigration, finances, and ideologies. Furthermore, our view of literacies (multiple and multimodal) as social practices opens up possibilities for seeing other (new and old) ways of reading and producing texts, including embodied texts in dramatic experiences and play. Our view of media as contexts—culturally produced and collectively maintained—creates avenues for exploring how players recruit and are recruited to, imagine, share, uphold, and wield these contexts in relation to other complex global and local networks of practice.

CONVERGING WORLDS, TRANSCULTURAL AND TRANSLOCAL LITERACY PRACTICES

Within the field of literacy there is an established body of work that addresses the relationship between global, transnational, and local literacy practices (e.g., Luke, 2004; Street, 2003; Albright, Purohit, & Walsh, 2006; Leander, 2001; Lam, 2006, 2007; Black, 2005, 2009; Guerra, 2008; Medina, 2010; Alim, Ibrahim, & Pennycook, 2009; Leander, Phillips, &

Taylor, 2010; Jimenez, Smith, & Teague, 2009; among others). In a review of promising research directions, Lam (2006) provides an in-depth analysis of the relationship among diversity, culture, and learning in the context of globalization. She highlights a significant body of research that focuses on diversity, literacy, and globalization in young people's experiences in contemporary times. In her concluding thoughts she argues that:

> Studying how social practices developed, how relationships are formed and indeed how teaching and learning take place in new digital landscapes and *other translocal contexts* would allow us to uncover the human processes behind our global conditions and the real opportunities and challenges of working with and for diversity in the contemporary era. (p. 232, emphasis added)

Gutiérrez (2010) suggests further directions in a review of the challenges faced in contemporary research in education that aims to understand the cultural flows within communities impacted by local, translocal, national, and transnational practices and the politics of access and marginalization embedded in these dynamics:

> We would want to study how practices travel, shift, or become hybridized in border and boundary crossing, or study what is learned in the movement across the practices of home and school, school and the corner, or across new media activity, for example, to account for historical, spatial, and temporal influences on an ecological niche. However, studying what takes hold in people's movement requires new sensibilities and tools, and new imagination about communities and their practices. (p. 487)

This book takes on the challenge of studying young children's literacy practices, relationships, and learning in their interactions with global networks and social conditions. We document how practices travel, shift, and become hybridized in people's interactions with global media networks in local communities, across activities, and in classrooms. We do so by examining communities and classroom practices such as play and dramatic experiences as literacy pedagogies that facilitate a space to make visible children's engagement with a large set of global and transcultural repertoires of networks and discourses. Furthermore, we situate our research narratives within complex and overlapping contemporary literacy research on transnationalism, transculturalism and globalization. This body of work can be broadly summarized in the following categories:

- Research on engagement and participation in global digital and media communities. This research includes youth engagement in online social networks and mobile technologies among others (Lam, 2007; Black,

2005, 2009; Lankshear & Knobel, 2006; Leander et al., 2010; Vasquez, in press; Vasquez & Felderman, 2012; Wohlwend & Lewis, 2011).

- Immigration, transnationalism, globalization, and mobility in relation to access, participation, and marginalization of language and cultural practices and the ideological and political dynamics of language and literacy practices across places (Jimenez et al., 2009; Blommaert, 2008; Campano, 2007; Guerra, 2008; Sánchez, 2007; Medina, 2010; Orellana, 1996; Enciso, Volz, Price-Dennis, & Durriyah, 2010).
- Sociolinguistic perspectives on flows of language across spaces, such as in the work in hip-hop studies and global Englishes (Pennycook, 2007, 2010; Alim et al., 2009).
- Impact of global and multinational media markets in children's literacy and interpretive practices as localization processes of these networks (Buckingham, 2003; Evans, 2005; Dyson, 2003; Wohlwend, 2009a, 2011; Mackey, 2003; Ito, 2007; Marsh, 2005b; Lemke, 2009; Marshall & Sensoy, 2011).
- The role of design in children's social futures particularly in relation to critical engagement with/in literacy practices foregrounding children's histories and engagement in local/global/transnational communities (Janks, 2009; Medina, 2006a, 2006b; Dockter, Haug, & Lewis, 2010; Baildon & Damico, 2010).

It is important to consider that these categories overlap and merge, such as in the work of Lam (2006), who examines Chinese immigrant youth and their engagement in digital communities; the work of Medina (2006a, 2006b, 2010), who examines immigrant children's literary engagement, including their interpretive discourses related to multinational Spanish media and translocal ways of knowing; or the work of Baildon and Damico (2010), who explore new literacies inquiry pedagogies in relation to multiculturalism, globalization, and consumption. As will become clear in the later chapters, we worked through play and dramatic experience to create complex social spaces situating what Appadurai (1996) defines as the role of the "imagination as a social practice" in contemporary society where the imagination becomes "a form of work" and "a form of negotiation between sites of agency" (p. 31), where improvisations are embedded in the creation of tools and discourses, such as designing digital tools for characters to communicate and problem solve; immigrant children's participation within their transnational repertoires of cultural and linguistic practices; consumption, adaptation, and production with/of global and multinational markets. These overlaps create contested and fluid worlds that complicate the artificial separation between global–local media and market relations, transnationalism and digital practices, and local–global politics. What is significant in this work is our attempt to understand that the local moment of engagement within play, dramatic experiences, and literacies is not a given but is always produced by the multiple localities children navigate and the histories and possibilities they bring to the creative moment. Therefore, movement and ambiguity "to expand the imaginative local outward" (Lewellen, 2002, p. 36), as anthropologists of globalization suggest, are at the core of the literacy pedagogies we share.

Furthermore we would like to also include a word of caution. Working in classrooms and doing research in communities at the intersection of children's converging worlds in play and dramatic experiences pose big challenges theoretically, methodologically, and pedagogically. In the work we present here, our goal is to examine convergences among the overlapping dynamics of local practices and a global landscape and to understand how these intersect with children's translocal moves, engagement with media, consumption of multinational markets and finances, and the ideological and hegemonic discourses that dominate as children move across these spaces. In order to avoid essentializing children's lives or assigning fixed meanings to the children's work we present, it is important to read this book as portraying the dynamics of meaning making as border crossings and juxtapositions. We focus on the ways these interrelated aspects of contemporary society converge in children's world at a particular place and time. Therefore, like any other anthropological approach to the study of culture, this book needs to be read as a partial text of children's lives and work in classrooms. In the next chapter, we describe our model of collective imaginaries to explain how we collaboratively reexamined the data presented in this book and how a multisited approach grounded in anthropologies of globalization, nexus of practice, and performative practices helped us frame our design and findings.

2 Understanding Multisited Imaginaries in Literacy Research

DEFINING COLLECTIVE AND MULTISITED IMAGINARIES

Throughout the previous chapter, we have used terminology such as *local, global, transnational, translocal, imagined communities*, and *imagined worlds*. In this chapter, we unpack some of these terms in relation to what we analyze as *collective imaginaries* and forms of scripting to see how children's playful and dramatic engagements in everyday social practices (such as classroom literacy practices) might make visible their relationship to contemporary global discourses and cultural practices. Figure 2.1 presents a visualization of our model for understanding cultural production and collective imaginaries. The notion of collective imaginary extends notions of "multisited imaginaries" (Marcus, 1998) and scapes from ethnographies of globalization (e.g., Appadurai, 1996), nexus of practice or webs of cultural practices that bind communities together (Scollon 2001), and identity as performative enactments that rupture existing social relationships and allow new ways of being to emerge (Goffman, 1974; Butler, 1990; Bauman & Briggs, 1990; Medina & Perry, 2014).

Work in anthropology and cultural studies has dedicated extensive efforts to defining people's relationship with globalization, transnational networks, flows of people, social goods, and information, including redefining what is meant by local imagined communities and imagined worlds. The implications of living in a historical moment where the relation between mobility and information seems to be key in describing social dynamics of access, participation, and marginalization pose new challenges to the traditional ways we understand bounded definitions of "local communities." The localities we physically inhabit are described in contemporary social research as blurred rather than bounded. In this body of research, new theoretical perspectives have emerged to make sense of the constructed nature of and permeability across nations and communities (Anderson, 1983; Appadurai, 1996; Marcus, 1995), including classrooms (Dyson, 2003; Leander, 2001; Wohlwend, 2009a). The work of Anderson (1983), while not initially intended to apply to globalization, generated a critical

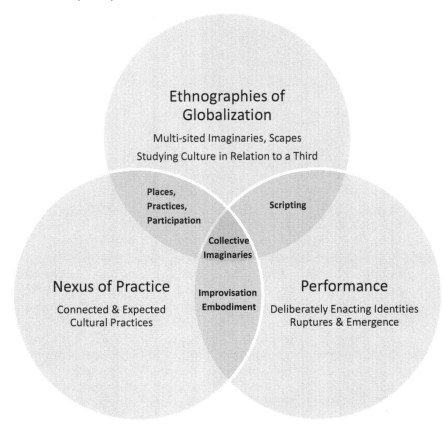

Figure 2.1   Model of collective imaginaries in contemporary times.

concept through his notion of imagined communities. In his critique of the "anomalies of nationalism," he makes visible the constructed nature of "the national" or "communities." He argues that histories of colonial power and selective hegemonic discourses interact through vernacular languages, print texts, and artifacts (what he calls "print capitalism") that serve to create mythologies that give the impression of communities as bounded social spaces based on colonial impositions. These mythologies create the illusion of bounded places that people call and embrace as nations or communities as we traditionally and historically know them. However, these constructions of community are also forms of exclusion that limit the scope of how and by whom culture is produced, and who gets to participate in that culture (such as in a dominant view of a unified U.S. culture in relation to White European values or in Puerto Rico's dominant ideology that cultural heritage comes mostly from a colonial Spanish culture). In his work, Anderson is not proposing that we should let go of the idea that localized contexts, knowledge, or communities exist or the idea that there are emerging social and cultural realities that exist within these. Instead, he establishes a difference between those who act within these "communities" to create and maintain a bounded sense of identity—either through colonial imposition or national rhetoric embedded in dominant ideologies that create a false and fixed definition of communities—and those who engage in collective acts of grassroots social action that redefine those social contexts into active forms of emerging and dynamic imagined communities. This fluid, imaginative, and active definition of the local informs our work as we wrestle with making sense of the porous nature of any locality. Thus, throughout the book we use phrases such as *local communities* to describe children's relationship with the physical locations and geographies in their immediate neighborhoods but with an understanding these are constructed, contested, and interacting with other imagined worlds that transcend physical presence. Naming and making visible these interactions in many forms frame our findings in significant ways.

The idea of imagined worlds comes from Appadurai's (1996) extension of Anderson's work to describe people's participation in global landscapes and the "multiple worlds that are constituted by the historically situated imaginations of persons and groups spread around the globe" (p. 33). It is at the intersection of these multiple imagined worlds and communities that new identities and forms of critical engagement could emerge in ways that Barnard (2009) describes as dynamics that "whether fixed in a particular locality or hypermobile . . . operate within a linked set of emerging global conditions" (p. 211). These global conditions are visible–invisible, jointed–disjointed, and integrated–"messy" across time and among people, places, and spaces.

The key question is: As social science researchers, and more specifically literacy researchers, how do we define and document the production of knowledge across boundaries and interpret the power dynamics that affect—or at least are made visible in—people's lives in local communities (including classrooms)?

ETHNOGRAPHIES OF GLOBALIZATION

Local–Global Networks as "Sites" for Cultural Production

Scholars in anthropology and the social sciences, such as Marcus (1995), Appadurai (1996), Bauman (1998), Blommaert (2005, 2008), Lewellen (2002), Castells (1999), Santos (2006, 2007), and Inda and Rosaldo (2008b), have argued that cultural production should be understood as transcending the limits of the local, repositioning knowledge in a globalized frame, where borders and flows of discourses are central to how researchers perceive people's identities and participation in local social and cultural practices. The work of those who study literacy and cultural diversity and how people live culturally, as Moll (2000) suggests, then becomes complicated by the ways people have access to and move across multiple landscapes (through media, migratory movements, new global economies, and technology) and how those landscapes interact, converge, and transform the immediate social contexts in which we live. Appadurai (1996) suggests that we live in a time where individual and group agency is located in the work of the imagination rooted in the "emerging 'spaces of contestation' seeking to annex the global into people's own practices of the modern" (p. 4). These global dynamics and flows are embedded in complex and contradictory consequences for different people and are not experienced in the same way across spaces and by all. Lewellen (2002) defines contemporary globalization in relation to local communities as "the increasing flow of trade, finance, culture, ideas and people brought about by the sophisticated technology of communications and travel and the worldwide spread of neoliberal capitalism and it is the local and regional adaptations to and resistances against these flows" (pp. 7–8) that make the consequences of globalization unique to each context. Furthermore, Ong (1999) argues that the "intermingling of spaces and practices of travel, production, discipline, consumption, and accumulation is a product of globalization, but its effects are apprehended, organized, and experienced in culturally distinctive ways" (p. 244). Therefore, conditions of globalization are always working in relation to the production of localities with specific consequences to each context. The interactions, mediated experiences, and consequences of people's access to and imposition of global flows and networks, according to Bauman (1998), means that: "What appears as globalization for some means localization for others; signaling a new freedom for some, upon many others it descends as an uninvited and cruel fate" (p. 2) with effects that are radically unequal.

Studying Culture in Relation to a "Third"

Culture in anthropologies of globalization is recognized as having many centers, and the construction and distribution of knowledge is perceived as emerging from multiple locations rather than one (Hannerz, n.d., 1996; Appadurai, 1996). This multiplicity of locations redefines the role of how both participants and researchers construct and contextualize places. Mobile reflexivity and agency (Marcus, 1995; Couldry, 2003) are then key to understanding that both ethnographers and participants are constantly working in relation "to a third," "a site elsewhere that affects, or even determines, their experiences and knowledges here" (Couldry, 2003, p. 47). We are making sense of spaces that interact simultaneously and that are complexly interconnected and where people participate in multiple habitats of meaning (Hannerz, 1996) to construct knowledge within and across locations. However, globalization cannot exist in the abstract and always functions in relation to a local. For Santos—who speaks of globalizations plural—the global always has roots in a particular local space and once in circulation is always produced in relation to other locals. He speaks of two modes of globalization:

1. "Globalized localism is the process by which a particular phenomenon is successfully globalized" (2006, p. 396). For example, Disney media for children promote a vision of Americana that originates in the U.S., but it is distributed through billion-dollar franchises in global markets.
2. Localized globalism that consists of "the specific impact on local conditions produced by transnational practices and imperatives that arise from globalized localisms" (2006, pp. 396–397). When children take up globally circulated media, they also consume its idealized messages. For example, Disney Princess depictions convey messages about beauty, thinness, and girlhood that can have dramatic localized effects and material consequences for children's developing notions of body image with long-term implications for their health and physical well-being.

The challenges to the epistemological and methodological uses of traditional forms of qualitative research, particularly ethnographic approaches, to understand and capture social relations and interactions in largely delocalized worlds have been explored in depth (see Marcus, 1995; García-Canclini, 1999; Kearney, 1995; Appadurai, 1996; Lewellen, 2002; Kraidy, 1999; in education, Leander et al., 2010; Lam, 2006). The body of research on the study of multiple aspects of globalization can be grouped in the following categories that are suggested by various authors in the anthology *The Anthropology of Globalization* (Inda & Rosaldo, 2008a):

- Ethnographic studies on media and globalization (see Murphy & Kraidy, 2003; Maira & Soep, 2005). Of interest to this book are ethnographies on telenovelas' reception and multinational media networks, such as Disney media production.
- Globalization, migration, and the politics of access and participation of refugees and diasporic communities in new contexts (Blommaert, 2008; Guerra, 1998).
- The impact of globalization in local communities with an emphasis on environmental and sustainability politics (Lewellen, 2002).

The work of cultural anthropologists such as Kraidy (1999), García-Canclini (1999), Hall (1996), and Hannerz (n.d.), among others, contributes to social science research a better understanding of how local everyday practices merge with global macro practices to perceive people's complex and contradictory relationship of new cultural and economic orders. Therefore, to think of how global landscapes interact with local practices involves understanding and mapping the interactions of the ways communities are constructed as bounded and/or permeable spaces in relation to how global networks are transformed, localized, and made dependent in very unique ways.

The challenging question though is: How do we study the material consequences of global corporate markets, media, and transnationalism without leaving out multiple overlapping experiences and knowledges that are too difficult to simultaneously map? Agency and mediation in this sense is acknowledged as fundamental in the study of globalization processes. In the process of negotiating micro and macro global discourses, "imagination as a social practice" (Appadurai, 1996, p. 31) is a key element in how people negotiate and interpret their encounters with global flows and networks to create new forms of social and political organization "that blend ways of knowing, ways of expressing and activism" (p. 177).

Places, Practices, and Participation

The local production of discourses then reflects ideologies that are massive in scale but that are re-created in local spaces through individuals' agentic participation and engagement with resources, including multimodal texts and artifacts such as media, print, technology, and so on (Soep, 2005; Maira & Soep, 2005). Studying these processes involves, as global anthropologists suggest, a "multisited imaginary" in ethnographic approaches to understand people's memberships across "sites," including what's defined as local communities with particular constructed histories, political ideologies, and mythologies (Anderson, 1983). These forms of membership and participation across communities and worlds translate into engagement with multiple forms of texts and social practices that have implications for how literacy researchers and educators understand the relationship between spaces as fluid and children's everyday experiences navigating multiple worlds (including classrooms) and texts.

Through our work, we aim to contribute literacy research to critical research of globalization in local communities that seeks to understand the production of global modernity and its impact to local processes (Kraidy, 1999; Kearney, 1995). Global media ethnographers Murphy and Kraidy (2003) posed a challenge, calling for new qualitative research practices that "develop more contextually grounded ethnographies while expanding the notion of the field to address the unique dilemmas of localized research in relation to the global issues raised by transnational media processes" (pp. 309–310). Using a multisited approach (Marcus, 1995) to data collection means that the researcher's fieldwork is embedded in searching for links and social relationships to other places or landscapes (Appadurai, 1996). *Places* and *landscapes* signal an understanding that what are defined as *communities* or *sites* are social constructs, created through people's discursive and imaginative ways of bounding particular spaces or imagined communities. In developing a framework for understanding contemporary dynamics of cultural locations or dislocations, Marcus draws on the work of Appadurai, among others, to reconfigure the notion of sites to landscapes people traverse and therefore ethnographers traverse in their fieldwork. Scapes, according to Appadurai, are "the multiple worlds that are constituted by the historically situated imaginations of persons and groups spread around the globe" (1996, p. 33). Defining what will become the object of study then "is designed around chains, paths, threads, conjunctions, or juxtapositions of locations, in which the ethnographer establishes some form of literal, physical presence, with an explicit, posited logic of association or connection among sites that in fact define the argument of the ethnography" (Marcus, 1995, p. 105). In the following chapters, we analyze situated classroom practices and document ways in which multiple worlds and markets interact in the immediate communities children navigate. We do so by documenting and analyzing how the multinational corporate flows of telenovelas and Disney media circulate and are made available to children. Making these cultural dynamics visible through elements of ethnographies of globalization, we then interpret children's mediation of these worlds in everyday pretend play and dramatic experiences in schools.

NEXUS OF PRACTICE: CONNECTED AND EXPECTED CULTURAL PRACTICES

To understand the tensions and convergences in global flows in relation to children's performative enactment, we draw upon Scollon and Scollon's (2003) theory of geosemiotics—a merger of intercultural ethnography, critical discourse analysis, and semiotics. Nexus of practice (Scollon 2001), a central construct in geosemiotics, is a group's intricate web of tacit insider practices, expectations, and dispositions. Nexus of practice explains how shared ways of meaning, doing, and being become attached to the ways we mediate and participate in imagined worlds and engage with global markets, renegotiated across transnational movements.

In this approach, any given literacy and media practice combines with other everyday cultural practices to form a nexus of practice of backgrounded naturalized ways of participating in a community. For researchers, this means that an individual action or a specific artifact cannot be decontextualized or analyzed in isolation. Instead, its locally embedded meanings must be understood as one point in circulations of global discourses and multiple histories that repeatedly converge and cycle through time and across space.

> Nexus analysis is a way of opening up the circumference around moments of human action to begin to see the lines, sometimes visible and sometimes obscured, of historical and social process by which discourses come together at particular moments of human action as well as to make visible the ways in which outcomes such as transformations in those discourses, social actors, and mediational means emanate from those moments of action. . . . our main point . . . is that a

nexus analysis, as a form of discourse analysis, can give us a fresh view of moments of social interaction and that such a view gives us leverage in bringing about change in the discourses that emanate from human action. (Scollon, 2002, para. 2)

To see how children are situated in global flows, it is necessary to discover the discourses and identities embedded in everyday practices with artifacts and trace the confluences of practices along histories and trajectories of interactions with these flows (Scollon 2001). In any classroom place, a complicated interplay of discourses, identities, practices, and artifacts shapes children's literacy and play interactions. Furthermore, these components interrelate in constitutive ways. Discourses are realized and submerged through the identities, practices, artifacts, and tools they legitimate:

- Identities and practices materialize in cultural artifacts and tools.
- Cultural artifacts and tools shape and are shaped by their users.
- Identities and discourses sediment over time into social practices.
- Social practices become routine and invisible in the nexus of practice in a particular place.

When a nexus of practice becomes the accepted, almost automatic way of doing things, it is integrated into each member's *historical body* (Scollon & Scollon, 2003), that is, the engrained sets of expectations and practices that make up habitus (Bourdieu, 1977) among a particular community. Nexus that accrue value over time within the collective social history of a group also serve as embodied forms of cultural capital (Bourdieu, 1986). When literacy practices and the symbolic capital they produce combine in a nexus, as in literacy play when children draw pictures and animate characters, the social and semiotic possibilities expand, making these nexus productive and potentially transformational (Wohlwend, 2008, 2009a, 2011, 2012).

Individuals learn to take up, and to want to take up, a culture's nexus of valued social practices (e.g., literacy practices, media practices, consumption practices, border cultural practices) as they engage in the world. In this interpretation of learning and development, children learn by participating in social practices in order to carry out real-world functions. As they engage in social practices, they also learn how to do things in the world to belong within discourses (Gee, 1996), or the tacitly valued ways of doing and being. These shared ways of talking about, interpreting, and justifying collectively valued practices strengthen a group's cohesion as well as individual members' connections to the group and to the discourse the group articulates. The performance of a valued practice is an embodied cultural marker that allows members to quickly recognize each other and to cooperate as group participants, whether as fans in a media affinity group, actors and audience, or teachers and students. In this way, a discourse is inextricably linked to its constituent practices as it circulates through the social practices it legitimates—naturalized practices that are often taught and learned implicitly (Scollon 2001). Prominent discourses around children's engagements in global markets and media include, but are not limited to, child innocence and vulnerability, developmentalism, neoliberal discourse, femininities and masculinities, and consumer agency (Blaise, 2005; Burman, 1994; Davies & Saltmarsh, 2007; Pugh, 2009; Wohlwend, 2009a). It is sometimes easier to see the nexus of practice operating in media discourses from the position of a fan. For example, to understand our own complicity in media discourses, we engaged in critical inquiry of the nexus of practice in hosts' and contestant's performances of postfeminist discourse around fashion and identity revision in the popular makeover cable television program *What Not to Wear*. (For the full analysis, see Appendix B.)

Discourses manifest through *identity texts*, material expressions that evoke a set of expectations for the performance of a widely circulated identity and suggest a routine performance and use of materials within a nexus of practice. Performances that meet these expectations facilitate quick recognition of that identity. For example, identity texts associated with accountability discourses in the nexus of practice in some school cultures are enforced explicitly through student handbooks and policy documents, classroom rules for managing bodies (good listeners sit still), report cards, guidelines for handling literacy tools (good students color neatly), routines for taking turns, and so on. Identity texts associated with discourses in media texts in the nexus of practice in consumer culture include character traits in film as well as film scripts and song lyrics, implied consumer attributes in advertising images and commercials, consumer affiliation with brand names, or anticipated player uses in toy designs and video games. Carrington argues that:

> The texts of consumer culture provide displays of available identities and lives. These texts are built around displays of style and taste, and children are being trained in particular patterns and knowledges around consumption. These texts are what they reflect—they are unashamedly commodities to be purchased and consumed, linked to the assumption of particular consumer identities. (Carrington, 2003, p. 94)

When media comes to school, as in the kindergarten in Chapter 5, classroom and family expectations mingle with consumer marketing and character identities in Disney Princess film narratives to make up the expected ways that boys and girls should interact during classroom play. In their interactions with media franchises, converging discourses construct children through various identity texts, such as *savvy consumers* and *vulnerable innocents*. In the space of school, the disjunctures among media and school identity texts spark a tension between children's desires as agents to freely express their media passions to form peer alliances in fan affinity groups and teachers' obligations to protect children from inappropriate or problematic content.

While identity texts are discursive, situated identities (Gee, 1996) are here-and-now subject positions in relation to other identities in a particular place. In this case, media discourses of consumerism and femininities in girlhood realized through the children's play practices constituted the situated identities Disney Princess fan and doll player just as educational discourses realized through writing workshop practices constituted the situated identities author, director, and actor.[1] During play, an identity text often resonates with other complementary or contradictory identity texts, creating a dynamic, multifaceted representation of self with meanings that may be imposed, unintended, or strategic.

Critical Scriptings: The Imagination as Social Practice in Play and Dramatic Experiences

Appadurai suggests that global flows are not located in an abstract space. Instead these are always mediated in local spaces, through concrete artifacts, activities, and experiences that translate into dynamics of indigenization and commoditization. These dynamics are described by Appadurai as scripting to make sense of the work of the imagination as a social practice in local communities. As individuals "experience" globalization in these local spaces, they can "re-script" their lives and localities in unpredictable ways. The work of Soep (2005) takes the notion of scripting to a concrete level to examine young males' local production of home videos and the gender performances that emerge in these productions. She argues that scripting is a way to understand "episodes of interaction" in the production of local texts and performances that foregrounds globalization and hybridity in youth engagement in everyday cultural practices. Borrowing from work in ethnographies of globalization, we use the notion of scripting as an interpretive framework to understand children's play, drama work and literacy engagement as cultural production. Scripting, or the role of the imagination as a social practice, works "as a way to understand episodes of interaction" in indigenization dynamics through the production of texts and performances that foreground the role of global landscapes in people's everyday lives. Soep suggests that scripting as an analytical tool offers a concrete approach to uncover how "national *imaginaries* and globalized *sensibilities* emerge in fleeting face to face encounters" (p. 176; emphasis in text) and to understand how culture is produced and interpreted as children perform complex social worlds.

Using scripting as an analytical lens allows for two things:

1. To interpret and resituate children as cultural subjects who can reimagine themselves and their worlds and experiences as they move across global landscapes.

2. To resituate children's ways of knowing outside the classroom as "aesthetic labor" productively engaged in working at the juxtaposition of texts, desires, ideologies, and the reformulation of cultural resources (media, written, and literary).

Furthermore, we were able to also examine how the productions of micro everyday practices are embedded in the macro-political ideologies of global landscapes. Studying these dynamics made visible how episodes of interaction are constructed in the production of local texts that foreground global landscapes such as the "shared discourses and semiotic repertoires that are glocalized in nature and linked to popular youth media" (Lam, 2006, p. 231). In Part II, we identify key aspects of critical engagement in analyzing children's scripting practices. In our analysis, we foreground the convergences and imaginaries constructed in performance as critical aesthetic labor. As young children engage in scripting, they are learning ways of belonging: to contribute to the cultural production enterprise of particular communities (classes, affinity groups) but also to collaborate in collectively imagining and sustaining that community. Communities are bound together by nexus of practice (Scollon, 2001) that mark members as insiders and that allow friends, fans, boys, girls, and so on, to mutually recognize each other as belonging to a shared imaginary. Furthermore, using scripting as way of framing and viewing literacy curriculum as cultural production helps us expand the ways interpretive dynamics are understood as people engage in local cultural practices that include negotiating global discourses, identities, and ways of social participation. In the next section we explore key aspects of performance as sites for cultural production (including play and dramatic experiences in classrooms) to relate notions of scripting and the imaginative work of children in their engagement with nexus of practice.

Embodiment and Improvisation in Playful and Performative Pedagogies

For us, the performative becomes an effective approach to working with children in their process of making sense of how culture is produced in contemporary times and how spatial forms are produced by human actions that are embedded in the politics of domination and resistance. Our definition of performative approaches to play and dramatic experiences comes from the overlapping tradition of works in critical feminist performance studies (Dolan, 1993; Diamond, 1996); feminist poststructuralist studies (Butler, 1990, 2005; Leander & Boldt, 2012); and critical performative pedagogies (Pineau, 2005; Medina, 2006a; Weltsek & Medina, 2007; Perry & Medina, 2011; Medina & Perry, 2013). In this work, *performativity* is defined as "the constructed nature of subjectivity, suggesting that social subjects perform themselves in negotiation with the delimiting cultural conventions of the geography within which they move" (Dolan, 1993, p. 419). Furthermore, Dolan argues that the creative works produced through theatrical performance practices such as classroom play and dramatic experiences could be considered as "located, historical sites for interventionist work in social identity construction" (419–420). We believe that play and improvised drama are potential spaces for the creation of relevant pedagogies that expose the complex dynamics of cultural production in relation to global–local worlds and the scripting practices produced by children in their everyday engagement with these multiple worlds. Within these dynamics in performance there are three elements that are significant in interpreting a performative moment: dynamics of cultural production, the acts of deliberately enacting and improvising embodied identities, and the emergence of ruptures and slippages in improvisation that allows for recontextualization and new discourses to emerge.

PERFORMANCE

Performative practices make visible how desires—including the desire to belong—shape children's interactions in converging worlds and with peers and affinity groups who share their passions. Visibility enables tracing the complicated interplay between children's popular media desires and gendered, raced, and classed scripts. Appreciating and foregrounding how desires shape childhood cultures enable recognition that we are more than consumers of media or other global flows; we are also active "producers" with opportunities for criticality, creativity, and agency as well as complicity in circulating practices, media, and discourses with disparate social effects.

In the process of making visible children's social practices and relationships with global flows in classroom literacy work, children need to be repositioned as engaged in aesthetic labor and cultural production. This perspective on critical engagement acknowledges that children participate in global landscapes as reflective agents capable of examining, redefining, and "playing with" the hegemonic and dominant discourses of globalization across the communities they navigate. As children's lives become mobile—even when they are physically in one place—the school literacy curriculum needs to become responsive to children's intercultural capital (Luke, 2004), not only to honor and foreground children's ways of knowing and engagement with global texts but to create localized spaces to make sense out of school social practices and power discourses that frame contemporary globalization politics.

Deliberately Enacting Identities

Play and dramatic experiences are immersive and self-aware, productive and deconstructive, playful and analytic. Dramatic pedagogies are visceral in a way that moves beyond print on the page; scripting reads bodies and writes with bodies to produce identity texts with sociopolitical meanings (see

Wohlwend & Medina, 2012, in Appendix B for an analysis of these dynamics). Identity then from a performative perspective is constructed, as Goffman suggests, as the social roles one performs in relation to "the enactment of rights and duties attached to a given status" (1959, p. 16) and the activities that encompass the presentation of oneself to an "audience." Furthermore, identity formation is understood, as Butler (1990) suggests, as constructed and constructing and working within and against the regulatory practices and discourses that aim to create a false or fictional stable self through "culturally intelligible grids" (p. 184) such as gender, race, socioeconomic status, and so on. The performative, then, is the result of and serves a purpose for public and social discourses that aim to maintain and disrupt identities within supposedly fixed cultural grids. When identities are understood as such, we are able to see the political constitution and the fabricated notions that frame hierarchies of power in identity constructs and how these are made visible in the performative moment. The contested nature of identity formation within media texts is apparent in our analysis of one contestant's performative disruption of the show's formulaic identity revision during a fashion makeover on *What Not To Wear* (see Appendix B).

We use the term *identity texts* to define the parts of scripts that structure roles and locate nexus, providing characters with recognizable storylines and players with stabilized set of expectations and actions. In popular media, our use of identity texts is a way of framing media narratives and consumer expectations that enables "critical examination of the complexity in children's play interactions with popular media artifacts as negotiations of identity and collaborative textual productions" (Wohlwend, 2012, p. 595). Expanded definitions of literacy now recognize a range of semiotic practices, including actions with artifacts as well as other aspects of multimodality. This moves the notion of text beyond verbal decoding and encoding of speech and print texts to include actions with bodies, objects, and images (Kress, 1997; Scollon, 2001; Scollon & Scollon, 2004; Siegel, 2006). Research shows that play (Wohlwend, 2008, 2011) and dramatic experiences (Medina & Perry, 2013; Edmiston & Enciso, 2002) are not only embodied literacies but also highly collaborative literacies that produce negotiated, coordinated, and enacted texts. This definition recognizes performance as an expression of text inscribed with bodies, for and with an audience, as an emergent text, constructed within the performance and influenced by the assumption of shared responsibility with an audience.

Media identity texts are not limited to verbal or written screenplays but include multimedia productions (e.g., television series, animated films, video games, websites) or artifacts (e.g., dolls, toys, clothing, or other consumer goods) that convey implicit and explicit messages about how children should act and who they should be and become (Wohlwend, 2009a). The forms of identity texts range from character actions, plots, and snippets of memorized dialogue that shape children's play to marketers' expectations for consumers in global markets.

Understanding media artifacts as identity texts allows us to extend our analysis to see children's performances in doll play or dramatic filmmaking as literacies of cultural production that read and write identities and that read and write the world. Identity texts are layered into artifacts along with shared meanings and literacy practices used to create or use the physical object. In this way, artifacts hold histories of prior identity performances associated with their creation or use. In using or wielding artifacts, social actors can evoke these sedimented echoes or histories of expectations (i.e., nexus of practice) in ways that stabilize their identity performances and link these to earlier events and meanings (Holland & Leander, 2004).

Walkerdine (1999) notes that performances of situated identities are site specific; here this means that classroom spaces influence the identity texts that children can access and perform. Childhood studies suggest multiple identity texts are available to children at play in schools, each justified, imposed, or circulated by a discourse that constructs and explains a particular vision of childhood, such as the natural innocence of childhood, the primacy of the individual, the agency of discovery learning, or the sanctity of free expression (Burman, 1994; Austin, Dwyer, & Freebody, 2003; Luke & Luke, 2001; Walkerdine, 1999).

Ruptures and Emergence

However, playful and dramatic encounters move a performed text or script to a new imagined situation, where it is recontextualized. To recontextualize is to replace the meanings of here-and-now of activity in physical environments with new meanings of an imagined context (Bauman & Briggs, 1990). Recontextualization transforms the setting but also transforms the identity texts that can be accessed and performed. Research by Medina and Perry (Perry & Medina; 2011, Medina & Perry, 2014) specifically addresses and analyzes classroom performance in relation to its potential to recontextualize and for new identities to emerge. Their analytical framework combines social theory and affective theory, revealing:

> the learner to be simultaneously inscribing and inscribed by social codes and cultural performances that get created, reproduced, and recontextualized in particular moments in time. This inscription occurs through engagement in activities and in relation to the multiple histories and subjectivities that performers bring to a creative moment (Pineau, 2005). In addition, we consider the affective dimension in these performance-based encounters. In this way, we consider the participant as a relational body/mind/self who through sensing, responding, and expressing is always becoming or "in motion" (Ellsworth, 2005) and creating new forms of participation. (Medina & Perry, 2013, pp. 116)

It is in the analysis of the interplay of what's there, what gets recontextualized, and the ruptures that emerge as new and transformational knowledge that they see much potential for performance pedagogies, such as play and dramatic experiences, in relation to what Butler (2005) suggests where: "certain practices of recognition or, indeed, certain breakdowns in the practice of recognition mark a site of rupture within the horizon of normativity and implicitly call for the institution of new norms, putting into question the givenness of the prevailing normative horizon" (2005, p. 24).

Furthermore, work in performance studies, particularly Bauman and Briggs (1990), suggest the notion of frames as widely accepted ways of organizing interaction among members of a culture. Frames shift realities (i.e., from classroom learning to pretense) through backgrounded keying (Goffman, 1974), a naturalized set of premises and signs that make all participants aware of a change in contexts (assuming they share an understanding of the rules of the nexus of practice). Children can change their classroom reality into a pretend family scenario by keying to a play frame through direct statements (e.g., "Let's pretend I'm the mother") or indirect actions (e.g., picking up a doll and cradling it, changing pitch to signal in-character talk) (Sawyer, 2003). In this way, play and dramatic experience enable access to imaginaries that would not otherwise be available in the current situation. Furthermore, these transformations create spaces for embodied critique: "play frames not only alter the performative force of utterances but provide settings in which speech and society can be questioned and transformed" (Bauman & Briggs, 1990, p. 63). Texts and contexts are inseparably linked, and need to be considered together; in the case of children's play and dramatic experiences, the message "this is play" is a text and a context, delivered simultaneously, that transforms the identities, actions, and materials in a here-and-now classroom to the characters, scripts, and settings in shared narratives that players collaboratively imagine into the classroom place. Play and drama frames laminate or allow multiple contexts to coexist in the same place: the physical realities and the imagined realities (Bateson, 1955/1972; Goffman, 1974; Leander, 2001). The transformative power of play and drama derives from this ability to recontextualize by decentering performances and resituating them socially and culturally as a single performance that indexes past and future events. For example, play and drama changes the set of underlying premises about identities, objects, and the immediate surrounding (i.e., a box is an empty container held by a child is a student in a here-and-now classroom) and replaces it with a new set of premises (i.e., "Pretend you are the queen and that box is your basket with the poison apple" [in the implied Snow White fairy tale]). This decentering or multiplying makes a new identity text plausible and interactionable, but the player's original identity remains as well. Pivots between the "real" classroom and pretended identity texts are easily accomplished as children step in and out of play as needed.

It is important to note that play and dramatic experiences are never entirely free of the original context, and this is significant for children's play in school settings. The coercive effects of institutional contexts as well as social relationships in peer cultures influence children's play (King,

1992). Children enact discourses and their associated ways of doing and being through play performances, responding to discursive constraints and opportunities through their play improvisations.

Recontextualization enables children to collaboratively engage imaginaries in a way that invites examination, critique, and makeovers. This active coproduction of contexts, texts, and interpretations during play makes content, framing, and roles visible and open to negotiation. "Contextualization involves an active process of negotiation in which participants reflexively examine the discourse as it is emerging, embedding assessments of its structure and significance in the speech itself" (Bauman & Briggs, 1990, p. 69). In play and dramatic experiences, actors are also audiences to one another's performances. Co-players actively interpret an actor's actions; these interpretations in turn affect the way that actors enact scenes or authors craft scripts. The notion of audience as coauthor recognizes that every utterance—or, as we argue, every embodied action—"is directed to and must be ratified by an audience" (Duranti, 1986, p. 243). Furthermore, actors anticipate and imagine audiences so that performances are always performed with an imagined audience; that is, we imagine how we appear to others.

SUMMARY

Here we pause to summarize some of the terms we've introduced and clarify how we see these elements relating to one another.

Play is a child-directed, transitory, and dynamic imaginative cultural practice. It is a participatory and spatializing literacy, informed by tacit understandings of cultural ways of doing things, that animates an unfolding narrative, dependent moment to moment upon a shared agreement among collaborating players to pretend together that the surrounding reality is somewhere else.

Dramatic experience is the threading of improvisational make-believe worlds that get constructed through writing, responding to texts, and/or acting and that get produced at the intersection of everyday experiences and imaginative practices (Edmiston & Enciso, 2002; Medina, 2006a, 2006b). Aside from its improvised nature, a key element in understanding dramatic experiences is that what happens, gets discussed, and created within and around an improvisation is essential to how knowledge is constructed.

Cultural production: Play and dramatic experiences are forms of cultural production that imagine a new context, importing an imagined space onto here-and-now places in global–local sites. Cultural production creates cultural settings or backdrops that make alternative scripts, nexus of practice, and identity texts relevant and actionable.

Discourse: A widely circulating monologue with legitimating language that justifies and upholds particular nexus of practice and community membership.

Identity text: A representation (text, artifact) that suggests an individual performance that fits a set of expectations within a nexus of practice for a particular identity and associated practices and routine uses of materials.

Improvisation: Deliberately enacting identities in "as if" scenarios, rupturing extant social structures, exploring these ruptures in embodied ways, and allowing new identity texts to emerge.

Nexus of practice: Webs of tacitly expected, almost automatic insider practices and dispositions that members of a group use as markers of mutual belonging. Nexus of practice influence who gets access and who can participate in a community's valued practices.

Pedagogy: A script that foregrounds a particular discourse (monologue) for the ways that cultural production is expected to unfold in sites, ostensibly schooling but many more. In this sense all pedagogies are scripts, but some are much more predictable and rigidly reproductive (i.e., "scripted"), while others are improvisational and productive by inviting alternative scripts to emerge through performance and play.

Place: A material (geographical, physical, and peopled) location that is simultaneously shaped and mediated by local and global practices to collectively produce cultural sites and communities.

Script (noun): Language but also action, materials, and practices that make up a vision of everything that we might expect to happen in a particular global–local site. A script connects multiple identity texts and puts them in relation to each other through a plan for the way actions, storylines, and identity texts are integrated into scenes (global–local sites).

Scripting (verb/action): Imagination as a social practice; that is, using drama and play as practices for imagining socially and culturally situated worlds, including "as if" worlds where alternative sets of premises make additional or contradictory identity texts possible.

Part II

Mapping Multisited Imaginaries in Literacy Research

To situate our research within the trajectory of works in anthropology of globalization, we had to open up our inquiries to new aspects, such as a redefinition of "sites." To make sense of what is meant by negotiating global–local relationships and its consequences to classroom literacy pedagogies, the global needs to be unpacked through examination that takes into consideration who, how, and what circulates as global–local converging dynamics with careful attention to situated local contexts. As we stated in Part I, the global is only relevant if understood in relation to local practices, cultural imaginaries, and politics. However, for many people "the local" is not only one place but the constant negotiation of meanings, cultural practices, and ways of knowing across many places, texts, and practices. Globalization cannot exist as an autonomous abstraction; it always functions in relation to one or multiple interacting locals or in relation to a "third" location that intersects with local community practices but originates in places outside the immediate community. The multisited nature of globalization is one of the guiding principles of this book.

Thus, we focus on the negotiation of meanings across places and spaces, or the construction of multiple habitats of meaning. Instead these are environments located across local–global landscapes through participation in global media networks, digital networks, and/or transnational/migratory repertoires of cultural practices. As in natural habitats, people give shape to and are shaped by habitats of meaning through successful participation that depends on their abilities to understand and interpret the forms of texts and discourses available to them within these habitats. But the questions that emerge from anthropologies of globalization are: How do we map the material availability of these texts, and how are these texts located, relocated, and integrated in people's everyday lives? This is the task we take on in Chapter 3: to engage in the mapping of the complex interactions and circulation of dominant global media in local communities.

Initially and similar to the design of ethnographies of globalization, the directions, "sites," or landscapes we needed to examine within our particular research contexts were not determined by us as researchers. Instead, during our observations in play, curricular experiences, interviews, informal dialogues, and so on, the children in our studies brought in their knowledge and experiences with global networks. We used their media interests and experiences as the point of departure for our fieldwork. We allowed paths and directions to emerge and embraced these, informed by Murphy and Kraidy (2003): "the situatedness of the local is not a site, place or space but rather a point of reference through which to engage dimensions of globalization" (p. 318). We also see this vantage point on networks as the initial and necessary exploratory step in a nexus analysis that maps the practices and habitats of meaning in a place:

> Nexus analysis begins where [global discourses are] enacted in the experience of real social actors. Then, after some detailed analysis of these actions, the analysis probes outward into the histories of actors, resources, scenes, or settings across time and place—first into the past to see how the actions are constituted and into the future to work toward shaping future actions. Thus the question of "Where do we start?" is answered quite directly: we start where we are and build out from there. (Scollon & Scollon, 2007, p. 619)

After mapping media flows across multisited networks, we turn our attention in Chapters 4 and 5 to classrooms where we then examine children's capacity to move, know, and make meaning across contexts through play and dramatic experiences. Play and dramatic experiences open a site within classrooms where we see potential to reframe literacy pedagogies from global and transcultural perspectives honoring and understanding how people and texts circulate within and across complex networks and practices in contemporary times, but to also understand the complicated politics of power and marginalization that are produced as a result of people's engagement with these contemporary cultural imaginaries. Within these imaginaries, children draw in familiar narratives from films, books, and television programs but also through the toys they love and the products they use. For example, media franchises circulate scripts for beautiful and powerless heroines in children's animated popular fairy tales or in melodramas in television programs. The narratives in these media circulate normative roles through global networks that, when played, align with expected practices, enacted and replayed locally among children who embody those imaginary worlds.

Play and dramatic experiences are also unruly and irrepressible. When media narratives and other related identity texts are enacted in children's play, their scripts mingle with on-the-ground cultural practices in ways that reproduce nexus of practice and remake social expectations. Here we ask: Can the imaginative power of play and dramatic experiences open opportunities for children to both impose and critique the accepted ways of doing things in classroom cultures? In our research and in our own teaching, we have observed that children may voice teacher-pleasing critiques of stereotypes in critical media discussions (Medina, 2004) but that deconstruction is often short-lived and ends at the classroom door; children maintained their media attachments and continued to uphold and impose gender norms in playgroups and on playgrounds (Wohlwend, 2007). In part, nexus for participating in classroom social worlds are structured by media affinities that create friendship bonds and group affiliations in peer culture (Corsaro, 1985, 2003; Corsaro & Eder, 1990).

In the next chapter, we first present an exercise mapping media imaginaries to demonstrate how while physically we "stayed" in one geographical location, we took a research stance searching for paths and the juxtaposition of scapes and locations that coexist in that geographical space and that were informed, brought up, and made visible in the community and more specifically by the students in the classrooms we were studying. In other words, by adopting elements of a multisited approach, we created a framework to understand the localization process of global flows and the new imagined worlds students become participants of. Furthermore, through a multisited approach to analysis, we can critically reflect on the implications of foregrounding the students' knowledge and engagement with global networks and discourses in relation to their lives and how those were made visible in their literacy work.

In Chapter 4, Carmen focuses on the strong intersection of ethnographies of globalization and the circulating telenovela identity texts in one community in Puerto Rico and puts this knowledge in relation to classroom literacy drama pedagogy in a third grade classroom as forms of scripting to make visible children's cultural production in the nexus of practice they navigate and the role of the imagination as a social practice as they make sense of worlds and discourses across locations.

In Chapter 5, Karen focuses on the intersections of nexus of practice in children's media play in a kindergarten classroom in Iowa, a largely rural U.S. Midwestern state. This chapter unpacks the slippages among nexus of practice as children perform and negotiate the meanings of "family" through Disney Princess play among girls and boys with transnational connections to other countries. The convergences of transnational, transmedia, and gendered nexus of practice produced tensions as the children played identity texts that conflicted with family cultural values or contradicted peer interpretations of gender roles in film narratives.

In Chapter 6, we look across these two research contexts to see how teachers and students negotiate their performative practices and cultural production of imaginaries, looking closely at clashes that emerge around what counts as knowledge and whose knowledge counts. We examine these convergences not only to see how these clashes occur but how they create new ruptures and the possibilities of expanded participation.

The questions in Figure II.1 frame a critical look at children's critical cultural production with telenovelas (Carmen) and Disney Princess (Karen) transmedia classrooms:

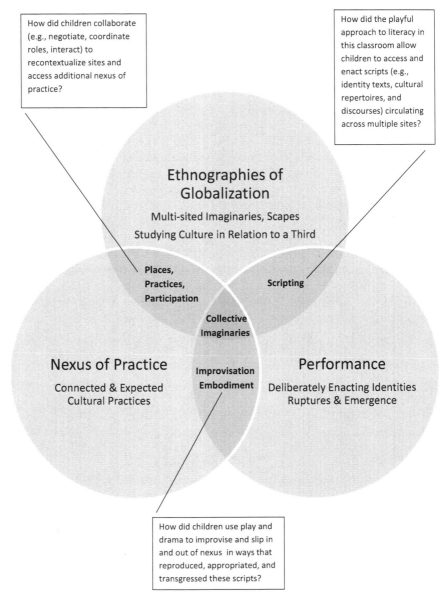

How did children collaborate (e.g., negotiate, coordinate roles, interact) to recontextualize sites and access additional nexus of practice?

How did the playful approach to literacy in this classroom allow children to access and enact scripts (e.g., identity texts, cultural repertoires, and discourses) circulating across multiple sites?

Ethnographies of Globalization

Multi-sited Imaginaries, Scapes
Studying Culture in Relation to a Third

Places, Practices, Participation

Scripting

Collective Imaginaries

Nexus of Practice

Connected & Expected Cultural Practices

Improvisation Embodiment

Performance

Deliberately Enacting Identities Ruptures & Emergence

How did children use play and drama to improvise and slip in and out of nexus in ways that reproduced, appropriated, and transgressed these scripts?

Figure II.1   Questions to locate critical cultural production.

3   Mapping Global Markets in Local Communities

Studying Cultural Production in Relation to a "Third"

TELENOVELAS AS CIRCULATING GLOBAL NETWORKS

In this section of the chapter, Carmen analyzes how telenovelas work as a global network in a moment of time within a community in Puerto Rico and the everyday interactions, including the continuum of engagement with telenovelas, as she moves back and forth between Puerto Rico and Indiana (her current place of residence). Within this analysis, Carmen explores telenovelas' markets as multinational media sites and the flows of images and discourses that are accessible through global tools and artifacts, such as television, Internet, magazines, and so on, in relation to its presence in the local community and beyond (see Figure 3.1). This analysis of the materiality of telenovelas in relation to local communities provides an understanding of how these media texts, as complex global networks, can be understood as a material and discursive mediascape (Appadurai, 1996), circulating and interacting in the immediate locality where the students live but also in interaction with other global–local networks and imagined worlds. This aspect of the analysis helps contextualize the students' work beyond the classroom boundaries and situates their work within frameworks of interaction that are part of their everyday lives but that transcend participation across spaces (real and imagined).

Telenovelas are melodramatic television series, sometimes compared with soap operas, but that only last around 150 episodes. Their origins are in Latin America, particularly Mexico, Venezuela, Argentina, and Brazil. Traditional themes include romance, relationships, betrayals, and power issues among its characters. More recent versions have incorporated contemporary themes, such as challenges to heteronormative sexuality or increased and sensationalized focus on drugs and violence. *La Reina del Sur* is a good example of a contemporary telenovela transformation actually based on a literary text. Similar to other global media phenomena, the beginning of these media shows can be traced back many years. Telenovelas have existed since the 1950s but presently are accessible to countries beyond Latin America and have become more

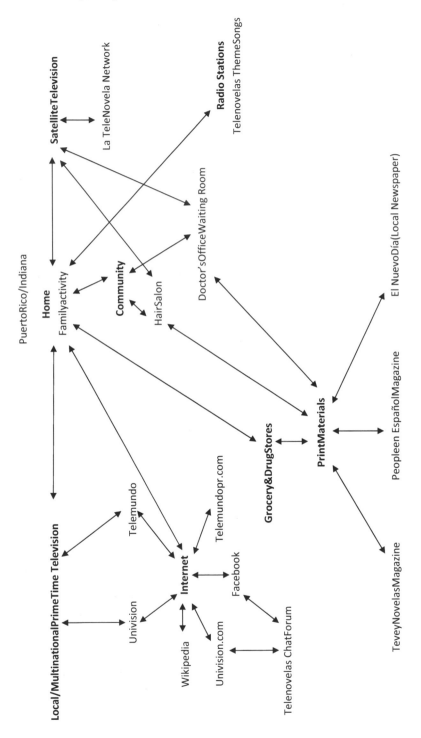

Figure 3.1 Mapping telenovelas' flows in a moment in time.

centrally produced by multinational companies in Miami as opposed to Mexico, Venezuela, or Puerto Rico, among others (see Mato, 2002, for an in depth analysis of telenovelas and globalization). They are described as a shared family entertainment activity that, according to Joyce (2008), becomes a forum for debate about people's private and public life as telenovelas bring "social models of gender roles, model relationships, organizational models for family and friends [that] are constantly being shaped and reshaped" (p. 3). Werner (2006) argues that telenovelas are successful among audiences given the "soft realistic way telenovelas deal with cultural difference and controversial issues" (p. 447). It is this simplistic approach to complex and controversial issues that becomes engaging for many telenovelas audiences, including children, although not all, probably most, telenovelas are not created with an intended audience of young people.

Telenovelas have also been described as cultural narratives where people across places participate in the consumption of and engage in the interpretation of a common media text (Orozco-Gomez, 2006). They constitute a multinational/global media market that reaches people across South and North America but also Asia, Africa, and Europe. In the U.S. and Latin America, with the spreading accessibility of Latino multinational networks such as Univision and Telemundo and the recent creation of La Tele Novela Network, viewers have access to a wide range of telenovelas choices 24/7 that range from old telenovela classics, such as the Mexican telenovela *El Derecho de Nacer* (The Right to Be Born), to contemporary ones, such as the Brazilian telenovela *Bellísima* (Gorgeous). The two major Latino networks in the U.S., Univision and Telemundo, provide blocks of telenovelas as their prime-time choices, sometimes starting at 5:00 p.m. and lasting until 9:00 p.m. In some ways it is quite challenging for Spanish-speaking audiences, who do not have access to cable television or who prefer Spanish-speaking television, to have other choices beyond telenovelas, particularly during prime time. The recursive process of demand and offer creates a media market that circulates between what viewers want and what corporate media believes sells. Furthermore, these dynamics make telenovelas a pervasive market that transcends the limits of the actual show through magazines (such as *T.V. y Novelas* and *People en Español*), websites, music, and tabloid television shows that highlight telenovelas actors' personal lives, such as *Al Rojo Vivo* and *Escandalo TV*, among others. These conglomerates of media networks become accessible to people in their local communities and create an imaginary space for shared participation and understandings. Telenovelas create habitats of meaning-making practices that circulate within and across communities and that emerge as places for shared understanding of common entertainment practices; each comes with its own set of dominant identity norms and power discourses. Participation in these habitats of meaning, according to Titley (2003), "suggests the need for strategies of orientation and the development of intercultural literacy in relation to the challenges posed by a globalising environment" (What's in a prefix? Section, para. 6). In other words, viewers of telenovelas develop ways of engaging with the meanings, structures, and overall composition of these media worlds in relation to other imagined worlds and their interactions with other people. People read, interpret, and participate in these media phenomena, reading across telenovela texts as cultural practices and in relation to the multiple other cultural locations people navigate.

As a hegemonic global phenomena, telenovelas have been perceived and analyzed from critical perspectives as perpetuating gender, economic class, and race stereotypes and viewers as passive consumers of these dominant stereotypical discourses (Meza, 2006; Romero as cited in Joyce, 2008). On the other hand, a postfeminist approach to telenovelas suggests that there is agency in viewers and that people do not passively consume these hegemonic media representations (Beard, 2003; Werner, 2006). The corpus of reception studies on telenovelas around the world is extensive and provides ways of looking and conceptualizing people's engagement, mediation, and responses to telenovelas (see La Pastina, 2003, for an analysis of these perspectives).

In the specific classroom project Carmen conducted in Puerto Rico, it became necessary to develop an understanding of how telenovelas circulate in the local community in relation to the cultural practices and imagined worlds children in the classroom engage in their everyday lives. It was important to document beyond the boundaries of the classroom the imaginary space for the creation of nexus of practices that promote a shared understanding or habitats of meaning where people engaged in watching telenovelas within the community where the study took place. This meant documenting how telenovela texts are localized and how they circulate across the community as a mediascape interacting with other local and global community practices. Using Marcus' (1995) work on multisited imaginaries in ethnographies of globalization, Carmen aimed to understand telenovelas as establishing "some form of literal, physical presence, with an explicit, posited logic of association or connection among sites" (p. 105). The mappings of these sites produced better understandings of the children's literacy work in the classroom and opened up possibilities for devising pedagogies that contextualize, recontextualize, and deconstruct these media texts. Furthermore, in the next section, Carmen describes and elaborates some of the complex social and political dynamics that frame globalization in the context of Puerto Rico and the communities around the school to explore how telenovelas add another layer or set of global–local interactions around the community and Puerto Rico.

Carmen, a Puerto Rican woman who currently lives in the Midwest U.S., spends a great deal of her time working with Latino/a children in communities in the U.S. and with Puerto Rican children in communities in Puerto Rico. This opportunity to move back and forth across educational and cultural contexts provides her not so much with a comparative view of educational contexts, but with an expansive view of how different classrooms and communities are transformed as new global networks and transnational dynamics (through people, economics, media, and digital migrations) impact people's lives. This is the case in the urban community of Santa Clara in Puerto Rico, where she works conducting research in a local elementary school. The present community of Santa Clara could be described as consisting of Puerto Ricans born and raised on the island, returning immigrants who move between Puerto Rico and the U.S. (sometimes several times and in very complex migratory cycles), and a large immigrant population from the Dominican Republic. Given that Puerto Rico is an official colonial territory of the U.S., the island has become highly populated with multinational corporate businesses that range from multiple fast-food chains, megastores (Walmart, Kmart, and Best Buy, among many others) and multinational communication services (Sprint, Verizon, AT&T, etc.), including multiple cable and satellite television providers (similar to the U.S.). These new multinational global dynamics create a consumer culture that has direct implications to people's relationship with media (print, television, digital, etc.), what sells, who consumes, and how it is consumed (Ortiz-Negron, 2007; Franco-Steeves, 2011), and that establishes complex identity dynamics of longing and belonging in relation to media representations of beauty, femininities, masculinities and socio economic status among many others. Although the community does have local businesses and services, its economic survival is in many ways contingent on the impact of new global business trends in the community. This is evident, for example, in the disappearance of local supermarkets in relation to the proliferation of Walmart, Costco, and Sam's Club multinationals. In many ways "progress" is perceived (particularly from a government standpoint) in relation to the establishment and development of multinational businesses on the island, although Puerto Rico cannot legally participate in any world trade economic initiatives. In this sense the island only serves to benefit multinational markets without any capital participation in these markets, something that can be conceived as a new form of colonial power (Bauman, 2007; Santos, 2006). To exemplify these dynamics, Figure 3.2 is a welcome sign, and an example of an illegal practice, of a nearby town on the northern coast of the island that reads, "Barceloneta capital del desarrollo economic" (Barceloneta capital of economic development). The sign includes a statement from the mayor, "Tabajando para mi gente" (Working for my people), surrounded by the logos of the multinational businesses established in the community. Within communities and government initiatives, global multinational networks become the impulse to create the illusion of a "nation" that is an active participant and benefits from global trends and economy.

Figure 3.2   Welcome sign in Puerto Rico.

Documenting these aspects is part of the ethnographic work Carmen does, providing an opportunity to be immersed in the everyday life of the community with her family, who have lived in Santa Clara most of their lives. These circumstances provide an opening to navigate through the community and to map how in her everyday life within the community telenovelas emerge in multiple locations as texts and discourses for consumption and interpretation. Figure 3.1 represents a map of Carmen's documentation of how telenovelas interact in the local community, including access to digital worlds. This figure is not intended to be interpreted as a generalization of a community interaction but as a mapping of one person's (Carmen's) experiences, interactions, associations, and connections with telenovelas across places during the time she spends in the community; in other words one set of paths, links, and juxtapositions of telenovelas with other cultural tools, resources, and practices.

There were multiple sites where telenovelas emerged as locations for interpretation and interaction. These included common activities, such as sitting down with her sisters to watch a telenovela. Every day from their respective houses, the sisters watch the most recent episode of the Brazilian telenovela *Bellísima* (Gorgeous). In this way, *Bellísima* became a common text, event, and the subject of conversations in family gatherings. Characters, plots, and tensions were explored and inferences made as we unpacked the events in the telenovela's episodes. Furthermore, it became an entertainment activity and a main subject of phone conversations with her family when Carmen returned to Indiana and continued to watch the same telenovela on La Tele Novela Network. The drama in the characters' lives, particularly in relation to economic power and how each characters' move was strategically crafted to affect those who were considered of a lesser status, framed their passionate conversations and inferences around what was happening and what might happen next.

Another site of Carmen's engagement with telenovelas in the community has to do with access to digital participatory communities. In the initial interactions with the students in the local elementary school (that Carmen further discusses in Chapter 4), the teacher and co-researchers had open-ended discussions about which telenovelas the students watched, why, and what made them so appealing to them. Children's responses—such as "porque tienen passion" (because there is passion), "porque tienen romance" (because there is romance), and "Hay villanos y hay buenos" (There are villains and good people)—gave us a sense of how the students interpret the social landscape of these media texts. They also spoke and compared their favorite telenovelas at that moment and mentioned titles such as *Muchachitas Como Tu* (Teenage Girls Like You; Univisión), *Un Gancho al Corazón* (A Hook to the Heart; Univisión), *Cuidado con el Angel* (Be Careful of the Angel; Univisión), *Al Diablo con los Guapos* (To Hell with the Handsome; Univisión). Carmen engaged in investigating more information about what these telenovelas are about and how they are presented to the audience. She quickly realized that the landscape of telenovelas goes beyond the actual television program. Table 3.1 exemplifies a summary of the information she found using as a focus the students' preferred telenovela, *Muchachitas Como Tu* (Teenage Girls Like You), which tells the story of four young woman who come together under very different social circumstances to create a pop rock group. Although, as the title suggests, they are supposed to live and be "como tu" ("like you"), the show is filled with stereotypes of dominant views of femininities, social class, race, and power.

Table 3.1   Sites of Engagement with Telenovelas

Telenovela	Content Summary	Samples of Sites of Engagement
Muchachitas Como Tu (Teenage Girls Like You)	Intended for a "youth" audience. Summary: Four girls who met at an acting school become friends. They get together to form a musical pop group. They come from different socioeconomic backgrounds, but their passion for music moves them to see "beyond" their differences. The story has multiple plots that deal with money and material acquisition, power, beauty, and materialism.	Summary of plot, history, links to actors web pages: http://en.wikipedia.org/wiki/Muchachitas_como_tú

Official telenovela website: http://www.esmas.com/muchachitascomotu/

Photos, chapters summaries, music downloads, chats with the actors, computer wall papers. |

(continued)

Table 3.1   (continued)

Telenovela	Content Summary	Samples of Sites of Engagement
	Although highly criticized, the last episode of this telenovela became the most watched episode in a telenovela in Mexico.	Review entitled: "Mexico TV Favors Light-Skinned Actors.": http://www.reuters.com/article/2007/08/14/television-mexico-dc-idUSN1338069320070814 (Reuters.com) Archive of episodes:www.youtube.com/watch?v=oko5HqvZBwY Official Facebook page: http://www.facebook.com/pages/Muchachitas-como-tu/115209925159035 Page to download official music theme: http://www.4shared.com/mp3/5WDCthFS/07_Muchachitas_como_tu_-_Belin.html

Similar to studies done on other television media phenomena (Buckingham, 2003; Wohlwend, 2009a), the range of information found about Latino/a telenovelas involves navigating multiple sites to locate a wide range of texts and information. These include Wikipedia, the official telenovela website, a range of YouTube episodes, a Facebook page, online newspapers reviews, and online magazines, among many others. Each site provides information and invites different forms of engagement that range from telenovelas fan chats, summaries, photos, music downloads, episodes, and reviews mixed with commercial advertisements of other products. All this information is available to multiple audiences around the world, including Puerto Rico. The local consumption of telenovelas gets expanded by the possibility of reading, writing, producing, and responding in digital spaces, engaging and connecting with fans around the world.

Local public spaces for engaging with telenovelas were also part of the experiences Carmen documented. For example, she documented that in public spaces, such as restaurants, hair salons, doctors' offices, and government agencies, television is widely accessible to customers and telenovelas are the show of choice. On visits to places like the hair salon, she could observe how clients' and employees' conversations revolved around the telenovela shown, becoming a common media text for interpretation and analysis. On a day when Carmen stopped by one of the local hair salons, clients (Carmen included) and employees watched the telenovela *Tormenta en el Paraíso* (Storm in Paradise), aired on Univisión. This commonplace activity turned into a conversation around the meaning of the title in relation to its content. *Tormenta en el Paraíso*, it was concluded, is a good title for the telenovela. The title, as it was unpacked by the group of viewers in the hair salon, relates to the rich male protagonist's hacienda or estate, named "El Paraíso," and to the ways the place was filled with problems and tensions after he married a "stormy" (troublemaker) woman. The "storm lives in paradise," affirmed this group of viewers. Here an interesting parallel emerges between the ways people "read" telenovelas and research that examines people's engagement with everyday out-of-school texts and practices in literary interpretation (Lee, 2007).

Similarly, multinational print-related texts, such as the magazines *Teve y Novelas* and *People en Español*, were frequently found both in public spaces and homes. Interestingly these multinational corporate magazines depend on and are attached to multinational television, creating interdependence among global markets. The more dramatic the characters' and actors' lives, the more material available to produce a successful magazine. During one of Carmen's home visits to a family member, she was able to browse through the subscription collection of *People en Español* that was available in the house:

> Hoy llegué a un hogar y veo en la mesa que habían recibido la revista *People en Español* en su edición especial "Los 50 más bellos." Luego de hojear la revista para identificar qué celebridades puertorriqueñas aparecían, comienzo a contar y me doy cuenta de que 17 de las 50 celebridades son actores de telenovelas: Thalía, Fernando Colunga, Lupita Ferrer, William Levy, Christian Bach, Saúl Lisazo, Jacqueline Bracamontes, Mauricio Ochman. (Field Notes, March 12, 2010)

> *Today I arrived to a home and I saw on the table that they had received the magazine* People in Spanish *and it was "The 50 Most Beautiful People" issue. After browsing to see which Puerto Rican celebrities made it onto the list, I began counting, and 17 of the 50 celebrities are telenovelas actors: Thalía, Fernando Colunga, Lupita Ferrer, William Levy, Christian Bach, Saúl Lisazo, Jacqueline Bracamontes, Mauricio Ochman. (Translation, Field Notes, March 12, 2010)*

In the above field note, it is possible to see the relation between telenovelas and the pervasive emergence of hegemonic discourses of beauty, class, and power that frame the representation of identities in telenovelas and their relation to how audiences access these discourses through the consumption of textual products. In this particular issue of *Los Mas Bellos*, 17 out of the 50 most beautiful celebrities were telenovelas actors, representing the largest number from a specific media and celebrity genre. Furthermore, within the magazines there were also multiple references to telenovelas, such as a special coverage entitled *Especial de Telenovelas: El Drama Detrás de las Cámaras* (Telenovelas Report: The Drama behind the Scenes), with photos, highlights, and special comments about telenovelas and their protagonists' lives.

Another aspect of telenovelas highlighted throughout these feature reports is the globalized nature of these media phenomena. In one article, "Drama Cibernético" (Cyber-Drama), there is reference to the emergent popularity of telenovelas in the U.S. According to this report, because many telenovelas are aired first in Latin America and then in the U.S., viewers in the U.S. go beyond the television media into digital spaces, such as YouTube, to watch not-yet-released episodes of telenovelas. As in the analysis of telenovelas websites, the magazines circulate in the local community, but the content situates the local reader within a larger transnational/global community of telenovelas fans. It establishes a bridge or a shared space for popular culture interpretative practices that is common across nations and Spanish-speaking communities.

The everyday encounters with telenovelas and their discourses in various places in communities make this media genre an important consideration in the development of new critical literacy pedagogies that transcend the limits of printed texts and attempt to engage children in an expansive view of multimodal literacies as social practices (Janks, 2009). Mapping how chains and convergences emerge in local communities provides a broader understanding of the complex habitats of meaning that the children in the study have access to, construct, and participate in.

DISNEY AS CIRCULATING GLOBAL NETWORKS

Like telenovelas, children's mediascapes are multisited, far-reaching flows that travel through everyday consumer products. Disney Princess transmedia is a prime example. The term *transmedia* (Kinder, 1991) describes franchises, anchored by films, television shows, or video games, with a reach that extends beyond multimedia to toys, books, video games, collectibles, apparel, and all sorts of household goods. These products link and circulate through identity texts embedded in the familiar narratives, characters, and logos that cover the products.

The Disney Princess franchise includes 12 Walt Disney Studios animated films: *Snow White* (1937), *Cinderella* (1950), *Sleeping Beauty*

(1959), *The Little Mermaid* (1989), *Beauty and the Beast* (1991), *Aladdin* (1992), *Pocahontas* (1995), *Mulan* (1998), *The Princess and the Frog* (2009), *Tangled* (2010), Pixar's *Brave* (2012), and *Frozen* (2013). The princess characters in these films are identity texts for girls (Snow White, Ariel from *The Little Mermaid*, Mulan) and women (Pocahontas, Sleeping Beauty), scripted femininities that are demure (Snow White, Sleeping Beauty), curious (Ariel), or plucky (Belle from *Beauty and the Beast*, Mulan, Tiana from *The Princess and the Frog*, Merida from *Brave*, Anna from *Frozen*). The animated fairy-tale worlds become globally available sites for imagining into local spaces, peopled by hyperfeminine characters who are deferent and above all kind to others as they overcome obstacles in their quests for good families, marriages, and happy endings (Davis, 2006; do Rozario, 2004; Giroux, 1999; Haas, Bell, & Sell, 1995; Walkerdine, 1984). For example, even the more active heroines, Ariel, Pocahontas, Belle, and Tiana, who save their heroes—or in the case of Mulan, her country—accomplish these feats through self-sacrifice and deference to a more powerful male (Lacroix, 2004). Furthermore, the Disney Princess storylines consistently feature problematic representations or elisions of gender, class, and race. By contrast, media reception studies and ethnographies of children's actual responses to popular culture find that children engage mediascapes with critical awareness (Buckingham, 1997; Davies, 2003; Dyson, 2003; Marsh, 2006; Seiter, 1993; Tobin, 2000, 2004).

In this book, we aim to recognize the pleasure, social bonds, literacy resources, and depth of emotional attachment that children get from engaging mediascapes such as the princess franchise. At the same time, we problematize the way the transmedia promote rigid gender categories through "conscious and unconscious desires, prepare for and proffer a 'happy every after' situation in which the finding of the prince (the knight in shining armor, 'Mr. Right') comes to seem like a solution to a set of overwhelming desires and problems" (Walkerdine, 1984, p. 163). The widespread distribution of the films through the Disney cable channel, DVDs, and other media outlets invites repeated engagements with a film's characters and storylines that build across movies, sequels, and spin-offs. This ensures that Disney Princess transmedia come preloaded with familiar storylines that are easily recognized, memorized, and replayed by millions of children (and their parents). To understand the depth of this connection, we need to understand the scope of Disney's top transmedia franchise.

The fairy-tale narratives in the 12 animated films and their spin-off DVD sequels make up just one site of engagement with the princess franchise. Disney Princess multimedia include digital forms such as e-books, video games, apps for mobile devices, MP3 audio, and an interactive fan site on Disney.com. Furthermore, multimedia comprise a small part

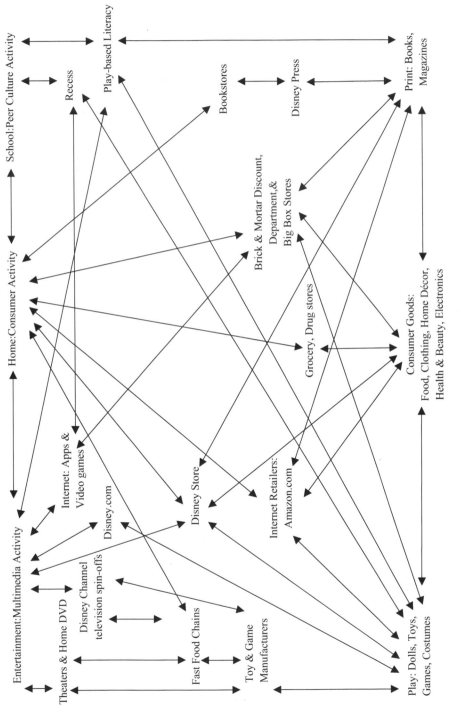

Figure 3.3 Mapping Disney Princess transmedia.

of the multibillion-dollar Disney Princess franchise. With $4 billion in annual global retail sales, the Disney Princess brand is a leading "lifestyle" franchise:

- The number one girls license toy brand in the U.S. among all girls and the number one toy brand for dolls and role play among girls ages 2–5.
- The National Retail Federation ranks Disney Princess among the top ten most popular holiday gifts for five years running.
- More than 142 million books, 81 million sticker packs, and 16 million Disney Princess magazines sold.
- Top ten in books category for *The Princess and the Frog* read-along app and top five paid book app for Princess Dress-Up: My Sticker Book app.

(Disney Consumer Products, 2011)

Disney Princess transmedia is distributed through an activity system of global consumerism that immerses young girls ages 3 to 6 in a flood of pink sparkly transmedia.

> We do not often enough realize that commercial marketing is the best financed source of media production in our world, and that it is often at the cutting edge of semiotic innovation, where we ordinarily expect to find only the arts (the least well-financed, if otherwise the freest). . . . Transmedia franchises place co-branded content, and with it their ideological messages and inducements to consumption, throughout our virtual and spatial environment, where our individual traversals will encounter it again and again. (Lemke, 2009, p. 292)

The 24/7 reach of Disney Princess transmedia ensures that children engage Tiana, Cinderella, Jasmine, and Snow White characters across multiple sites in a single day: from screens to stores to playrooms to bedrooms to classrooms. Princess dolls and collectibles stashed away in book bags and pockets emerge during recess, where they enter as capital into peer cultures on school playgrounds.

In rural places in the U.S., such as Iowa, transmedia sites of engagement intertwine with commercial marketing and distribution transactions, which are increasingly on websites such as Amazon.com or in regional discount stores or their websites rather than in brick-and-mortar shops in local neighborhoods. As local chain stores close, merge, or migrate to larger population centers, residents who live in rural towns rely on Internet and cable services to consume popular transmedia. Rural residents in geographically isolated locations can still access the same websites as urban dwellers, although their access depends upon the robustness of broadband connections (e.g., speed, reliability, capacity) and the affordability of shipping costs. An expanding variety in online consumption exists alongside a shrinking list of local retail outlets as brick-and-mortar store sites are determined through corporate decisions about sales potential and target demographics. The range of available products in local stores is also increasingly subject to similar marketing expectations. In this way, rural consumers' everyday shopping choices are shaped by the available stock on the shelves of a handful of large ubiquitous chains that intentionally locate in rural areas (e.g., Walmart).

About a decade ago, when Karen was working in Iowa schools as a kindergarten teacher, she noticed a growing trend: from year to year, the girls in her classroom were increasingly fascinated with Disney Princesses in the toys they shared, the clothes they wore, and in their classroom play and writings. Surveying the aisles of an Iowa Walmart, Karen found Disney Princesses—among other popular media characters—decorating an array of children's goods. Predictably, Disney Princess products included girls' nightgowns, sportswear, and other clothing, pillows and comforters, birthday party goods, and beauty products but also SpaghettiOs, bikes, Band-Aids, light-up sneakers, crayons, glitter, markers, high chairs, and a "princess potty." This sampling aligns with Disney's current list of merchandise licensed with the brand's signature pastel pink packaging:

- Home—bedding, room decor, furniture, fine art, collectibles
- Stationery—back-to-school supplies, party goods, seasonal
- Food, health, and beauty—personal care, vitamins, beauty, meals, and snacks
- Publishing—activity, coloring, craft and novelty books, storybooks, magazines
- Soft lines—apparel, footwear, sleepwear, and accessories
- Toys—arts and crafts, dolls and doll accessories, dress-up and role-play, games and puzzles, novelty, play sets, ride-ons, and sporting goods
- Consumer electronics—MP3 players, digital cameras, and personal DVD players (Disney Consumer Goods, 2011)

The identity text in a pink Disney Princess T-shirt sold at Walmart is gendered (pink, lace, and embellished font signal girls-only) and classed (products offer low price and mass-market appeal). This means that the merchandise that young children in rural stores are most apt to see will often symbolize an affiliation with a single, nonnegotiable gender. In this way, engagements with everyday products incite discourse (Foucault, 1978) by requiring constant decisions as children choose between binary and fixed categories:

- In Walmart's color-coded toy aisles (pink and pastel packaging for girls, black and metallic for boys).
- In the drive-through window at McDonald's (the order taker asks, "Do you want the boy toy or girl toy?" which is encoded in print on the LED readout as "truck toy" or "doll toy").

- Among the vitamins on the end caps at the corner drugstore (two choices: Disney Princess Gummies or Marvel's Heroes Gummies featuring Spider-Man, Ironman, and Captain America).
- In the soup and snack aisles in the local grocery store (Campbell's Disney Princess Soup or Disney/Pixar Cars Soup; Kellogg's Disney Princess or Mario Brothers fruit-flavored snacks).

Children's intense attachments to hyperfeminine Disney Princess transmedia have sparked controversy over the identity-shaping potential of gender stereotypes and beauty ideals. Parental concern spawned recent mass-market books, *My Princess Boy* (Kilodavis & DeSimone, 2010) and *Cinderella Ate My Daughter: Dispatches from the Front Lines of the New Girlie-Girl Culture* (Orenstein, 2011). However, a child's emotional attachment to princess products is not organic or accidental; this is love by design. In order to establish an emotional bond with target consumers, marketers design a "brand identity": casting their inanimate products as "brand as person" so that consumers interact with an imagined person rather than a functional product (Aaker, 1996). The brand persona communicates particular traits that a user might want to emulate while the brand–consumer relationship anthropomorphizes the product as an interactant, making "Levi Strauss a rugged outdoor companion; Mercedes-Benz an upscale, admired person . . . and Hallmark a warm, emotional relative" (Aaker, 1996, p. 84).

The princesses in the Disney Princess films provide the foundational personalities for the franchise's brand identity, merging the 13 heroines[1] into a brand persona that is a friendly, lovely, and loving deferential ingénue whose primary end goal is to attract the hero. The brand identity emphasizes the glamour of the princess role and reduces the individual heroines' storylines to variations in their hairstyles and dress styles (Wohlwend, 2009a). What remains is a distilled hyperfeminine persona, a set of narrow beauty ideals (e.g., long flowing hair, White, thin), and passive roles in romantic storylines (Giroux, 1999; Haas et al., 1995). It is important to note that there is elision as well as essentializing of race and ethnicity at work here: Mulan and Pocahontas rarely appear on product packaging. A cursory search of Amazon.com shows that the most frequently depicted princesses on food, health, and beauty products, party goods, valentines, home decor, and so on, are Cinderella, Sleeping Beauty, Snow White, Jasmine, Belle, and Ariel. Tiana, Disney's recent addition of an African American princess, appears on some newer packaging, as much an indication of the character's popularity as a response to critiques of the lack of diversity in the Disney Princess brand (King, Bloodsworth-Lugo, & Lugo-Lugo, 2010; Lee, 2009).

The brand identity also creates a brand–consumer relationship: the brand as a lovely, loving royal friend and role model that positions young girls as adoring fans and princess wannabes. The brand-consumer relationship manifests through everyday use of shampoo and lunch bags, as identity kits that make the Disney Princess imaginary omnipresent, tangible, and highly available to preschool girls, the market demographic. These branding practices anticipate girls (only) as the appropriate consumers and fans for the Disney Princess franchise through advertising that shapes expectations among female consumers and princess players. As consumers, children participate locally in worldwide networks of distribution and consumption through multiple activities with Disney Princess products: purchasing licensed merchandise at discount stores, drugstores, grocery stores, or online retailers, displaying favorite dolls and wearing related clothing, or viewing princess multimedia on television, in theaters, on the Disney.com website, and on DVDs at home (see Figure 3.3).

Children's homes are key sites of engagement with Disney Princess transmedia, through daily interactions with products purchased for them by their families. Parents recognize and often support young fans' attachments to popular transmedia (Marsh, 2005b; Pugh, 2009); as a result, parents are the indirect targets of commercial toy marketing to children. The franchise also appeals to nostalgic memories of parents and grandparents who watched the fairy tale films as children, expanding brand recognition across generations and generating more sales. In 2011, Disney was the top-selling media franchise, with total sales of $1.6 billion in North America and $3 billion globally (Goudreau, 2012). The storylines and characters that underlie these popular products carry discourses (Gee, 1996)—naturalized ways of interacting according to widely circulating, tacitly held beliefs—that shape what counts as appropriate ways to be and belong: in this case, idealized models of girlhood associated with the Disney Princess brand that depict how children should enact girls, players, and consumers, among other identities.

Dramatic play and playful storytelling in early childhood classrooms provide another site where children engage Disney Princess media flows when teachers enact a "permeable" literacy curriculum. Similarly, telenovelas flow into classrooms when media are recognized as resources and children are encouraged to draw upon their culturally diverse linguistic repertoires through performance pedagogies. In the following chapters, we explore how children engage transmedia flows in classrooms in Puerto Rico and in Iowa.

4 Cultural Production of Telenovelas' Dramatic Worlds

Carmen Liliana Medina and
María del Rocío Costa

LAS BELLAS VAN AL DIABLO

Había una vez una mujer que era bella y una fea que la mando al diablo. La bella se sintió triste de lo que le había dicho la fea. La mujer fea se reía, "Ja, ja, ja."

La mujer linda se encontró con un hombre que era novio de la fea y la mujer linda se enamoró del hombre rico. La mujer pudo casarse con el hombre rico.

La boda se había iniciado. Ella le dijo al novio "Tu novia de antes me dijo, vete al diablo" Entonces la mujer fea detuvo la boda y la mujer linda lloró y lloró porque no se pudo casar. Estaba decepcionada porque el hombre le había dicho que no tenía novia. La linda vino y saco una navaja, la mató y se pudo casar con el hombre rico y pudieron vivir felices para siempre. (Students' devised telenovela. First draft.)

Once upon a time there was a woman that was beautiful and there was an ugly one that sent her to hell. The beautiful one felt sad because of what the ugly one had told her. The ugly woman laughed, "Ha, ha, ha."

The beautiful woman ran into a man that was the boyfriend of the ugly one and the woman fell in love with the rich man. The woman was able to get married to the rich man. The wedding had already started. She said to the boyfriend, "Your girlfriend from before told me to go to hell." Then the ugly one arrived, held up the wedding, and the beautiful woman cried and cried because she could not get married.

She was disappointed because the rich man had told her that he did not have a girlfriend. The beautiful one came and killed her with a knife and was able to get married to the rich man and they lived happily ever after. (Translation. Students' devised telenovela. First draft.)

On the surface the above students' devised telenovela. *Las Bellas Van al Diablo* [The Beautiful Go to Hell] might seem like a simple text written by a group of third graders in a classroom in Santa Clara, Puerto Rico. From a writer's craft perspective, a generic and perhaps a set of under-developed characters and plot could be one way of looking at this text. Nevertheless, a closer reading of the nuances involved in the composition of this text magnifies the children's performance (almost like a satire) in their representation of social discourses and the construction of identity texts in telenovelas. Like most satires, the text is crafted in a way where playful production and improvisation involves the process of knowing, deconstructing, and remaking cultural and social representations that are complex. The children construct and maintain imagined worlds, drawing from a familiar narrative as they have access to it through multiple media discourses. In this case what this group makes visible is their participation in a nexus of practice where multiple telenovelas and the children's immediate worlds intersect. Their engagement in the process of scripting emphasizes the objectification of gender roles in the creation of characters that are only named and defined as "la mujer fea" (the ugly woman), "la mujer bella" (the beautiful woman), and "el hombre rico" (the rich man), in the normalization of violence without consequences, and in the passion and betrayal relationships explored in the text. The children's imaginary world of a telenovela is an exaggerated version of almost the multiple normative identities they encounter in their everyday lives watching television in Spanish and more specifically telenovelas.

In the next sections, Carmen and María del Rocío share their collaborative work with the classroom teacher and a group of third graders in an urban public school in Puerto Rico. Through a critical inquiry approach (Lewison, Leland, & Harste, 2008; Medina & Costa, 2010), the students self-selected the topic of telenovelas to explore in the classroom. The overall aspects of the experience included an analysis of the content and structure of telenovelas, reading literature resembling or disrupting the structure of telenovelas, producing and performing telenovelas, and a critical analysis of the social discourses brought in the students' production. After the work on telenovelas was complete, we designed a unit analyzing beauty and consumption discourses in the media, an issue that emerged as a result of the telenovelas inquiry experience.

This work took place as part of a larger four-year ethnographic study conducted with co-researcher María del Rocío Costa from the University of Puerto Rico, Bayamón Campus. We worked collaboratively as a teacher-researcher team (Whitmore & Crowell, 1994) with two teachers in a second and third grade classroom. Given Puerto Rico's colonial condition, schools follow and are regulated through the same federal mandates, such as No Child Left Behind or the Common Core Standards, in combination with a set of local standards similar to what each state in the U.S. has but with a focus on Spanish literacy instruction. Local and imported commercial programs are mostly used and one program is usually adopted by the entire island as a common literacy curriculum. Given the homogenization that results from these mandates and textbook adoptions that have been largely unsuccessful, in our project we aimed to investigate the implementation of a literacy curriculum grounded in children's out-of-school social practices and its potential for the development of a student-centered critical literacy curriculum. We worked with the children in multiple cycles of inquiry that resulted in a permeable curricula (Dyson, 1993), where students' experiences framed classroom literacy work. Because the topics emerged from the students, we engaged a wide range of topics, such as those related to popular culture like telenovelas and superheroes. These then turned into critical inquiries on gender and media, and real-life heroes and social justice issues. We also worked on a unit on violence and tolerance in their communities that then evolved into a family inquiry project on social issues that mattered to members of students' families. This inquiry opened up a number of topics, such as local violence, immigrants' rights, gay and lesbian rights, child abuse, and animal abuse, which were then explored in small groups. We also used the students' ideas in a writer's workshop that focused on the students' voices rather than on mastering a sequence of genres. Although different genres were explored, including their technical aspects, the students' ideas led our explorations. In this workshop approach, the students worked both individually and in collaboration, exploring a wide range of topics and ideas, including the integration of action figures, photography, and other multimodal explorations to generate stories for writing. In this sense there was openness in how we perceived the "how to do" literacy in the classroom and how we worked beyond individualized models of literacy toward collective creations and explorations (for detailed descriptions of these activities, see Medina & Costa, 2013; Medina & Perry, 2013).

When we dealt with the topic of telenovelas in the third grade classroom, we faced the challenge of engaging with a media genre that is not necessarily intended for children, although it is traditionally viewed as a family activity. This posed challenges but also opened possibilities in designing a literacy curriculum from a critical social practice approach. One of these aspects was the process of keeping at the forefront an openness to examine global media texts in ways that acknowledged viewers rapport with and their desires and pleasures in watching telenovelas. Similar to Buckingham's (2003) work on media reception, we understood that people, including the students and ourselves, enjoyed watching telenovelas but also criticized and found them problematic; therefore, our approaches to these explorations had to be framed with this in mind. We worked on finding ways to use the children's and our own experiences to critically reflect on the dominant identity texts and discourses of power embedded in these global media phenomena while accepting telenovelas as possible texts in the classroom, where other nexus of practice children have could merge, new identity texts could emerge, and other social realities could be improvised. This was a complicated task; it also created conflicting, contradictory, and productive decisions and approaches to our work. The following section is specifically framed around the questions presented in the introduction of Part II of the book:

- How did the playful approach to literacy in this classroom allow children to access and enact scripts (e.g., identity texts, cultural repertoires, and discourses) circulating across multiple sites?
- How did children collaborate (e.g., negotiate, coordinate roles, interact) to recontextualize sites and access multiple nexus of practice?
- How did children use drama to improvise and slip in and out of nexus in ways that reproduced, appropriated, and transgressed these scripts?

SCRIPTING GENDER PERFORMANCES IN CONVERGING SPACES BETWEEN LITERATURE AND MEDIA: COORDINATING AND NEGOTIATING MULTIPLE NEXUS OF PRACTICE

The interaction presented below occurred after the students had spent some time engaging in open discussions around different aspects of telenovelas. We discussed content, preferences, structures, and themes. The teacher and researcher's goal was to listen to children's understandings and meaning-making processes regarding telenovelas as performed identity texts and spaces with unique elements and structures that created an affinity group among the children as media fans of telenovelas. The students' responses showed that they had a complex understanding of these media texts, including the hyper-sensualized identity texts and the dynamics of social power represented in the stories. The following transcript was part of a literature-media discussion in which, as part of the inquiry project, the students and teacher read the Spanish version of the *Paper Bag Princess* (Munsch, 1991). The curricular engagement was meant to interpret telenovelas through a literary text in order to work in a hybrid space between in- and out-of-school literacies.

[ ] Clarification Text
( ) Overlapping speech
. . . Pause

[Maestra Vivian reads section on *Paper Bag Princess* where Ronaldo rejects the princess.]

Transcript	Translation
Manuel[1]: Como en *Un Gancho al Corazón* hay una mujer que entra a una oficina a pedir trabajo y viene una secretaria y le dice que no puede trabajar ahí porque estaba vestida con una facha.	Manuel: Like on *Un Gancho al Corazón* [A Hook to the Heart] there's a woman that goes into an office to ask for a job and a secretary comes and tells her she can't work there because she was dressed with a *facha* [like a mess].

(continued)

Transcript	Translation
Maestra Vivian: ¿y eso es otra [tele]novela?	Maestra Vivian: And that's another telenovela?
Manuel: [*asiente con la cabeza*]	Manuel: [*nods yes*]
Javier: ¿Misis y que es una facha?	Javier: Mrs., what does a *facha* means?
Rocío [co-investigadora]: ¿Qué es una facha?	Rocío [co-researcher]: What does a *facha* means?
Maestra Vivian: ¿Alguien sabe?	Maestra Vivian: Does anyone know?
Carlos: Que estaba vestida fea.	Carlos: That she was dressed in ugly clothes.
Maestra Vivian: ¿Y cómo estaba vestida ella?	Maestra Vivian: And how was she dressed?
Manuel: Con un pantalón cortito que parece una falda y un traje bien pega'o	Manuel: With shorts that looked like a skirt and a really tight dress.
Carolina: [Conexión inaudible con *Muchachitas Como Tu*] Misi' como en *Muchachitas Como Tu* . . .porque Federico solo se fija en las riquitas por como se ven [inaudible].	Carolina: [inaudible connection to *Muchachitas Como Tu*] Mrs., like in *Muchachitas Como Tu* . . . because Federico only looks at the rich girls because of their looks [inaudible].
Carlos: Maestra en lo del príncipe el le dice que . . . porque como se ve sucia pues parece que el no la quiere.	Carlos: Teacher, in the story about the prince he tells her that . . . because she looks dirty it seems like he doesn't love her.
Maestra Vivian: ¿Se ve fea por qué? ¿Por qué?	Maestra Vivian: She looks ugly because? Because?
Carlos: Parece que es pobre.	Carlos: She looks like she's poor.
Maestra Vivian: ¿Parece que es pobre? Y si es pobre no la quiere y si es fea no la quiere. Eso pasa en las [tele]novelas.	Maestra Vivian: It seems like she's poor? And if she's poor, he doesn't love her and if she's ugly, he doesn't love her. That happens in telenovelas.
Manuel: Si. *Como en Al Diablo con los Guapos*. Que estaba una mujer que se llama "Mili-gol" y a ella no le importaban como se veían los pobres y cada vez que iba visitarlos les limpiaba, daba comida, sabanas . . .	Manuel: Yeah. Like in *Al Diablo con los Guapos* [Down with the Beautiful]. There was a woman that was named Mili-gol and she didn't care what poor people looked like and every time she went to visit them, she cleaned for them, gave them food and sheets . . .
Josue: [inaudible referencia a un personaje rica] Era muy orgullosa pues se convirtió en pobre entonces después cuando fue Mili a darle comida, sabanas y ropa pues le dijo la muchacha que la llevara a la casa.	Josue: [inaudible reference to a rich character] [The rich character] she was really prideful and she became poor and so when Mili went to give her food, sheets, and clothes, the girl asked Mili to take her home.

(continued)

Transcript	Translation
Maestra Vivian: Ah en esa novela *Gancho al Corazón* una persona que era rica y se volvió pobre.	Maestra Vivian: So on the telenovela *Gancho al Corazón* [A Hook to the Heart] a person that was rich became poor.
Josue: En *Al Diablo con los Guapos*.	Josue: On *Al Diablo con los Guapos*.
Maestra Vivian: En *Al Diablo con los Guapos*.	Maestra Vivian: On *Al Diablo con los Guapos*.
Manuel: Y en *Al Diablo con los Guapos* hay una mujer que vivía en una mansión y que era rica y entonces ella despreciaba a Mili porque ella antes era una sirvienta.	Manuel: And *Al Diablo con los Guapos* there is a woman who was rich and lived in a mansion, but she treated Mili badly because she used to be a servant.
Maestra Vivian: Había rechazo también.	Maestra Vivian: There was rejection too.
Manuel: Si, y después ella por rechazarla, [a Mili] este le vino lo malo y se volvió pobre porque el esposo de ella, pues nada el la dejo porque estaba loca y bebió mucho y la llevo a una una. . . .¿a la casa de los locos?	Manuel: Yes, and later because she rejected her [Mili], then the bad came to her [popular saying] and she became poor because her husband, well, left her because she was crazy and she drank a lot and he took her to the, to the . . . the madhouse?
Rocío [co-investigadora]: Al manicomio.	Rocío [co-researcher]: To the asylum.

One of the aspects we wanted to explore was how to bring literature and media together in the classroom literacy curriculum. Because the content of telenovelas' narratives has been compared and in various cases has been inspired by Cinderella-type stories (such as the telenovelas *Floricienta* [*Flower-ella*] and *Lola: Erase un Vez* [*Lola: Once upon a Time*]) and the students' explorations of telenovelas were highly charged with hegemonic global discourses of beauty, we decided to introduce a different kind of Cinderella story through the reading of the *Paper Bag Princess*. Although we understood the criticism of this kind of feminist approach to literary texts (Davies, 1993), we still found possibilities in bringing another kind of discourse to widen the range of femininities and masculinities that were brought up in the discussions. We were aware of the risks embedded, particularly in relation to the teacher selecting and imposing a "gender script" on the students, but we also understood that from a performative pedagogy standpoint, any "script" generated or presented by teachers is already embedded in power discourses and the historical layers of authoritarian performances that are inscribed in teachers' identities. Introducing a traditional Cinderella story would perhaps have hidden our subjective positions in relation to the students' beauty discourses on telenovelas, but hidden or obvious, those positions are still circulating.

What became interesting through the analysis of this transcript were the students' acts of redefining the media-literary as a nexus of practice where the valued practices of literary response and media response permeated but also were rescripted and improvised. Similar to Davies (1993) findings of children's interpreting feminist texts, the students did not "hear" the same kind of feminist text that we heard in *Paper Bag Princess* (1980). Rather, in an agentic move as media and literary consumers and producers of meaning, they created a different kind of interpretive space, disrupting a vertical approach to critical interpretation (telenovelas at the bottom and authoritative critical/literary interpretation at the top) into a more horizontal plane or a landscape to "script" and make interpretations across the multiple global telenovelas, literary, and gender imaginaries within a repertoire of stories with situated meanings and complex identity text performances. Their ways of interpreting made visible multiple nexus of practice where we can map the lines in which multiple discourses come together in telenovelas, allowing us to understand the process of emergence and materiality of "echoes of global power" (García-Canclini, 1995; Murphy & Kraidy, 2003, p. 15) in their work that hinted at the active negotiation of media authority by the students not situated in one text but in multiple texts that are brought up in nonlinear or sequential manner.

In the above transcript, Carlos begins with a connection to the telenovela *Un Gancho al Corazón* [A Hook to the Heart]. *Un Gancho al Corazón* is the story of Valentina, a nice beautiful young boxer who is trained by her abusive and controlling boyfriend, who wants to make money by exploiting Valentina. Valentina eventually meets her "true love," a young rich man, but he is engaged to a mean and selfish woman. After overcoming obstacles and challenges in their love, Valentina and the rich handsome male live happily ever after. Power, class, betrayal, and romance are among the main discourses framing the story. In his first statement, Carlos makes a connection to this telenovela by highlighting the relationship between class and global hegemonic discourses of beauty and power. He makes the relationship visible when he sees acquiring a job as contingent upon physical appearance. Furthermore, his use of the descriptor "facha" (raggedy and messy clothes) situates his statement within popular everyday lingo used to describe people who are not dressed appropriately.

Carolina then makes a connection to the telenovela *Muchachitas Como Tu* [Teenage Girls Like You], a title that indicates that the characters' identities in the telenovela resemble those of the viewers ("they" are/look like "you"). *Muchachitas Como Tu* is the story of four girls from different backgrounds (although all light-skinned, thin, and with the type of beauty that responds to global norms) and their journey into becoming a popular pop group. This telenovela was highly criticized in

Mexico for its overrepresentation of light-skinned characters and lack of representation of characters from indigenous backgrounds, but it was still highly popular among young audiences from all ethnic backgrounds and across countries. This light-skinned phenomenon has been described as a global trend in telenovelas (Hecht, 2007) and one that recreates dominant cultural grids of feminine identities (Butler, 1990), but that does not seem to necessarily interfere with its popularity among young audiences from multiple ethnic backgrounds. Its active audience included the children in the classroom involved in the present study who selected this telenovela as their favorite, mostly because of the complex desire or longings created by new global media trends of youth popular culture, such as shows that glorify how "everyday" girls could become celebrities and popular media stars (Marshall, 2011).

Carolina, who did not fit the beauty and size standards of women in telenovelas and who made this clear at some point in the inquiry process, was the first girl to comment on this interaction: "Misi como en *Muchachitas Como Tu* porque Federico solo se fija en las riquitas por como se ven." [Mrs., like in *Teenage Girls Like You* because Federico only looks at the rich girls because of their looks.] She names and interprets the identity discourses related to the male characters' desires for beautiful females of affluent socioeconomic status. What is not clear is whether the telenovela generated a discourse of socioeconomic status and beauty that suggested that all rich females have a particular look or if males only like rich females who looked a particular way. This utterance hints at the complex ways in which forms of beauty construct socioeconomic status and how socioeconomic status constructs forms of beauty. Either way, Carolina's participation as a critical reader of the media text indicated her awareness of how gender identities were interwoven in relation to socioeconomic status, beauty, and power within telenovelas. A short time later, Manuel brought up the second global telenovela, *Al Diablo con los Guapos* [To Hell with the Handsome]. A nexus of practice is made visible when the students connect with each other to make sense and move across multiple imagined worlds in relation to the localized and normalized discourses of power and gender that get constructed. The title of this media text indexes a more complex and contradictory identity meaning in relation to positioning the content and its audience. *Al Diablo con los Guapos* suggests a discourse counter to traditional views of telenovelas in which female protagonist characters passively fall in love and glorify handsome males. *Al Diablo con los Guapos* suggests a move to reject the male-dominant beauty discourses that are often found in telenovelas. Nevertheless, a careful examination of the students' responses creates a more complex map of how beauty discourses circulate and were interpreted through this telenovela in ways that moved beyond rejecting beauty.

Manuel began to unpack the contradictory social landscape of this telenovela by telling his classmates and teachers about "Mili-gol's," the protagonist's, story: "Que estaba una mujer que se llama Mili-Gol y a ella no le importaba como se veían los pobres y cada vez que iba a visitarlos les limpiaba, daba comida, sabanas." [There was a woman named Mili-Gol and she didn't care what poor people looked like and every time she went to visit them, she cleaned for them, gave them food and sheets.] Mili's identity is interpreted as an outsider to lower socioeconomic communities. Although she was presented in previous episodes as coming from a low socioeconomic background, she eventually "overcomes" poverty and becomes rich and an active helper and protector of those who remain in poverty. In Manuel's analysis of Mili's social performance, people who are "poor" are presented as disempowered or passive, where Mili actively did things "for them." Those "things" Mili does go beyond providing food and include "cleaning for them," which suggests a relationship between sanitary care, disempowerment, and people of lower socioeconomic status. Furthermore, in Manuel's interpretation, Mili, who at the end of the telenovela marries the rich and handsome protagonist and who herself fits the beauty canon of telenovelas, helped poor people because "she didn't care what poor people looked like." Manuel's position as interpreter of global media discourses was similar to Carolina's interpretation of *Muchachitas Como Tu*, as he made visible the interrelated politics of socioeconomics and beauty identities, where in telenovelas, poverty constructs ways of looking and ways of looking construct poverty. In Manuel's statement, Mili moved beyond poor people's ways of looking to help them in their struggles with poverty, defined by goods and neatness. Furthermore, Josue's follow-up to Manuel's comment introduces another layer of performed power and economic status discourses through the story of the "rich woman" antagonist who "was really prideful and she became poor." Here, Josue adds to the previous idea of economic poverty and appearance in relation to power performances that suggest poverty is a punishment for inappropriate individual behavior. The "rich woman" became poor as a result of mistreating Mili, who was previously poor but eventually became rich. What the students' comments made clear was their active meaning-making processes in relation to telenovelas as fairy-tale narratives in which performed identity discourses suggest that good behavior gets rewarded with material wealth and beauty and bad behavior is punished with material poverty and "ugliness."

These excerpts were part of a much more complex interaction among students and teachers, but they capture how children read, interpreted, and were aware of the situated meanings and how identities across telenovelas texts echoed discourses of power within this particular global media genre. The next excerpt shows another aspect of the dramatic experiences in telenovelas.

SCRIPTING GLOBAL IMAGINARIES AND LOCAL SOCIAL CONDITIONS IN NEXUS OF PRACTICE: PERFORMING WOMAN IN STRUGGLE

As part of the classroom engagements, the students worked in small groups, designing and producing telenovelas. The range of texts the students designed and the repertoire of themes and resources that they used were quite expansive. As shown through the following excerpt, the students' designs became hybrid products in which participation in multiple nexus of practice where meaning-making practices and identity texts merged and were key in the locality the students created in their telenovela designs (see photos from children's telenovelas in Figures 4.1–4.3). The following script is a child-produced telenovela script by a group of girls who decided to write the story of a family whose mother was in a fight with the father and asked him to leave the house and he refused to do so.

Sin Corazón No Hay Amor	*There's No Love without a Heart*
[Mamá]—Yo estoy feliz y vivo con mi esposo y con mi hijo y mi hija que acababa de nacer.	[Mother]—I'm happy, and I live with my husband, with my son, and my daughter, who was just born.
[Papá]—¡Dame a mis hijos!	[Father]—Give me my kids!
[Mamá]—¡No son tus hijos! ¡Yo los parí!	[Mother]—They are not your kids! I gave birth to them!
[Narrador]—Mientras los papas peliaban los niños lloraban.	[Narrator]—While the parents fought, the kids cried.
[Papá]—¡Son mis hijos1 ¡No son tus hijos!	[Father]—They are my kids! Not yours!
[Mamá]—¡Yo me quedare con ellos!	[Mother]—I'm going to keep them!
[Narrador]—Los niños lloraban y lloraban hasta que lo niños querían decidir quedarse con uno de los dos.	[Narrator]—The kids cried and cried until the kids wanted to decide to stay with one of them.
[Mamá]—¡Vete de la casa ahora!	[Mother]—Leave the house now!
[Narrador]—Y los niños le dijeron a la mama.	[Narrator]—And the kids told their mom.
[Hijo/a]—Mami, ¿y donde se quedará?	[Child]—Mom, where is he going to stay?
[Mamá]—Papi ya no es tu papá.	[Mother]—Dad is not your father anymore.
[Hijo/a]—¿Por qué papi no se va a quedar en ninguna casa?	[Child]—Why is Dad not staying in any house?

(continued)

Sin Corazón No Hay Amor	*There's No Love without a Heart*
[Hijo/a]—¿Por qué el ya no vive con nosotros?	[Child]—Why isn't he living with us anymore?
[Narrador]—Y la mama de los hijos se sintió mal porque, porque no vive en ninguna casa el papá	[Narrator]—And the kids' mom felt bad because the dad did not live in a house.
[Mamá]—Niños me siento mal porque su papá no vive en ninguna casa.	[Mother]—Kids, I feel bad because your father is not living in a house.
[Mamá]—Niños, ¿Quieren quedarse con su papá y conmigo?	[Mother]—Kids, would you like to stay with your father or with me?
[Hijo/a]—Si mami si queremos volver con papi	[Child]—Yes, Mom, we want to go back with Dad.
[Mamá]—Lo voy a llamar. ¡Tu estas borracho! ¡No lo puedo creer! ¡No volveré contigo!	[Mother]—I'm going to call him. You are drunk! I can't believe this! I'm not getting back together with you!
	[The story continues and the mother eventually forgives the father and lets him come back home.]

Figure 4.1 Children's telenovela performance: *Sin Corazón No Hay Amor/There Is No Love without a Heart* hospital scene.

Figure 4.2   Children's telenovela performance: *Sin Corazón No Hay Amor/There Is No Love without a Heart* parents' argument.

Figure 4.3   Children's telenovela performance: *Sin Corazón No Hay Amor/There Is No Love without a Heart* parents' reconciliation.

This performed telenovela was produced as a meaning-making site of complex aspects of social life at the intersection of everyday experiences, identity texts, and the structures of mediated culture. The imaginative social worlds, identities texts, and practices between global and local discourses (scripting) were at the core of how this performance was produced by the students. The characters' encounters became a hybrid set of local–global echoes between one of the girl's personal testimonies and the identities, discourses, and structures of telenovelas. The students were dealing with conflicts of gender and power, and while this text should not be perceived as a literal representation of the student's life, attitudes, or dispositions (for a critique of this kind of claim, see Buckingham, 2003), it was informative in examining how children understand their everyday worlds and make visible the gender and class nexus and the identity texts and structures in media productions. What was important in this analysis was the children's cultural and social production and the performed identities that were constructed within this fictional world as potential entries or ruptures into a more complex analysis of how global and local meanings intersect (an analysis of ruptures will take place later in the next sections).

The overall structure of the telenovela uses *Cinderella* as an identity text with both implicit and explicit sedimented histories in which the female character encounters a problem or challenge related to a male partner that gets resolved in the end, when they live "happily ever after." The text follows what telenovela scholars define as the three structural elements of this media genre (Werner, 2006): (1) characters live a stable life, (2) an event occurs that disrupts this balance and creates a number of other hardships, and (3) finally, balance is achieved and happiness restored. For the most part, this is the overall traditional structure of telenovelas and one that was mostly used by all the students in the classroom. Children's performances of characters, although agentic and unique, are also constrained by the identity texts provided by traditional telenovela structures and global power in the creation of gender roles. These form a complicated set of subtleties that are revealed within the texts and that are significant to unpack. These subtleties can be understood as part of a media performance that functions as a resource to produce and make visible the "*mediation* of social life" (Couldry, 2003) in relation to power relations, agency, and emotional investment or as a nexus of practice where the children's insider's practices as viewers and interpreters of telenovelas are negotiated in relation to their participation in other social worlds that converge to create characters, plots, and actions.

Take, for example, how motherhood was constructed (see script sections in bold). One of the overall features of this text was the mother's tone as exclamatory. Throughout the children's written text, her voice was represented with exclamation marks, highlighting the expression of both emotions and actions in her statements. After she gave birth to her third child, the father, for an "unknown" reason, told the mother to give him the children. Her reaction to this statement was to claim that the act of childbirth gave her rights over the children. She decisively refused to give the children to the father and in an agentic move she asked him to leave the house. The children, who expressed their relationship with the father through emotions that were visible in their sadness as they witnessed the situation, complicated the mother's role. The mother firmly acted to get the father out of the house, but, emotionally, she felt conflicted because of the children's concerns about the father not having a place to live and because they missed him. Agency was mediated in the mother's story through her actions and emotions, creating a complex map of social life within this telenovela representation. After consulting with the children, the mother made the decision to allow the father back in the house, but, to her surprise, he was drunk when she called him. Once again she reaffirmed her decision to keep the father away from the house, but eventually there was a final forgiveness and they "lived happily ever after."

This telenovela production was accompanied by the students' musical selection of the song "Masoquismo" by the Latina teen pop artist Lola from the album *Erase Una Vez* [Once Upon a Time] that actually served as the theme song for a popular telenovela. The lyrics of the song, about a woman who was left by her lover but feels conflicted in her emotions and calls herself a masochist, becomes another imagined world in a complex nexus of practice that complements the main theme of the students' script. This telenovela production and the previous literature-media discussion became performative spaces to both analyze and produce meaning within the structures of global media texts. The students' generative literacy work created new parameters for creating a new nexus space to interpret global media structures and local social realities but where ruptures are created for new meanings and ideas to be improvised and to emerge. The following script exemplifies one of the group discussions analyzing photographs of the students' performed telenovela *Sin Corazón No Hay Amor* [*There Is No Heart without Love*]. The students are discussing the possible motivation for the conflict and the father's departure.

Discussion	Translation
Alicia: Porque la mamá quiere comprarle esto y el papá no esta dispuesto a comprarle eso.	Alicia: Because the mother wants to buy something for the kids but the dad isn't willing to buy it.
Marcos: Ah verdad, o el dinero.	Marcos: True, or money
Javier: Este los papas, la mama necesita chavos porque no tiene para los hijos y el papá dicen que no le va a dar.	Javier: Well, the parents, the mom needs money because she doesn't have any for the children and the father said he won't give it to them.
Rocío: Y ¿por qué? y ¿por qué? Yo tengo una pregunta con eso . . . que me quede así como que sorprendida. ¿La mamá le tiene que pedir chavos al papá?	Rocío: And why, why? I have a question about that . . . that left me like surprised. The mother has to ask for money from the father?
Marcos: Si no tiene.	Marcos: If she doesn't have any.
Carlos: Si, también le tiene que pedir por la pensión.	Carlos: Yes, also if she has to ask him for child support.

In this instance it is possible to see the hybrid identity discourses that emerge by "freezing" and analyzing a moment in time. Here, the role of the spectator and performer merge as children contemplate and enact the remaking of the mother in struggle and that in relation to an economic struggle. It is at this intersection of identity, discourse, and politics that we see much potential in media and critical literacy education. The students' work was not about finding some kind of unified or single oppressive discourse in relation to media; instead, it was about generating or critically scripting new layers of identity and social performance that work as reflective spaces of complex and overlapping power dynamics in relation to beauty, class, gender, economics, childhood, and relationships.

In addition, teachers and researchers reflected on these nexus of practice as they made curricular decisions. The following section presents an analysis of a planning moment among the teachers and researchers to demonstrate how our roles and performed identities shifted as we worked at the intersection of global media, students' and teachers' identity work, and discourses.

RUPTURES IN GLOBAL–LOCAL CONVERGENCES: MEDIATING CURRICULUM DESIGN BETWEEN LOCAL AND GLOBAL LITERACY IMAGINARIES

The inquiry on telenovelas posed multiple challenges to us as a team of teacher-researchers. These challenges related to not only the specific approaches we used to work collaboratively with the children but also our curriculum design process as a teaching team. As we delved deeper into the complex landscape of global media texts in relation to gender and children's identity work (both in the real and fictional worlds), a number of ruptures began to emerge that complicated our planning work and that became a set of interesting reflections on critical literacy, design, and the materiality of global–local forces.

In the following instance, the classroom teacher, Maestra Vivian, Carmen, and Rocío met to reflect on the telenovela inquiry and to decide on a second cycle of inquiry based on the students' responses and our reflections on the previous telenovela projects. At this particular point, we were trying to decide if an inquiry on dominant media beauty representation was the best approach for the second inquiry cycle. We were looking at the collection of student-generated work on telenovelas and discussing ways to create a new inquiry framework to work at the intersection of the media social landscapes produced by the students and everyday identity performances and power, particularly beauty and gender. The following transcript shows a planning moment when the teacher, Maestra Vivian, decided to share a note from Alicia, a girl in the classroom. In this note, Alicia shared feelings about her personal appearance in relation to her participation in school social spaces.

Transcript	Translation
Maestra Vivian: Yo tengo algo que me entregó Alicia.	Teacher Vivian: I have a note that Alicia gave me.
Rocío: [*making reference to beauty as the possible topic for inquiry*] La pregunta es ¿hay que conectarlo con lo de las novelas?	Rocío: [*making reference to beauty as the possible topic for inquiry*] The question is, do we have to relate [the new inquiry] to the telenovelas work?
Carmen: No	Carmen: No.
Maestra Vivan: Esto [el discurso de la belleza] salió en las novelas cuando exploramos de que se trataban las novelas y ellos hablaron de que eran bonitas. De que las muchachas eran bonitas de que le gustaban etcétera pero no creo que lo tengamos que conectar con las novelas. [*leyendo del papel que le entregó Alicia*]: "Nadie quiere se mi amigo y yo no se y todo el mundo no me hace caso porque soy gorda. La única amiga es Carolina."	Teacher Vivian: These ideas [the beauty discourse] emerged on the telenovelas when we explored what telenovelas are about, and they said that they [women] are beautiful. That the girls are beautiful, that they like them, et cetera, but I don't think we have to connect it to the telenovelas. [*reading from a piece of paper Alicia gave her*]: "No one wants to be my friend and I don't know and no one pays attention to me because I'm fat. My only friend is Carolina."
Rocío: Que también es gordita.	Rocío: Who is also overweight.
Maestra Vivian [*continues reading*]: "y me siento triste y todos los nenes me dicen lechona y yo trato de defenderme."	Teacher Vivian: [*continues reading*] "And I feel sad and all the boys call me a hog and I try to defend myself."
Rocío: Lo que a mi me preocuparía de esto es que no se transforme en algo como a bregar con nuestros problemas internos porque yo creo que ninguna de nosotras está preparada para trabajar con los problemas internos. Lo que hay que ver es por qué nosotros tenemos estos problemas internos. Porque cuando tu entiendes: "No soy yo. ¿Verdad?. Es esto que está allá afuera." Que si yo tan solo veo mujeres flacas entonces por eso es que me siento como me siento y eso es lo que está mal no yo.	Rocío: What concerns me about this is that it doesn't turn into something like how to deal with our inner issues because none of us is prepared to work with inner issues. What we have to see is why do we have those inner issues? Because when you understand: "It is not me, right? It's what is out there." Like if I only see women who are skinny then that's why I feel the way I feel and that's what's wrong and not me.
Carmen: Claro, entonces por ese lado utilizar lo de las telenovelas crea esa distancia.	Carmen: Of course, from that perspective, using the telenovelas creates a certain distance.

In this interaction it is important to notice how the decision-making process in designing an inquiry cycle based on beauty and media became contingent on Alicia's perceptions of identity performances framed by the local dominant beauty discourses represented in her note. Alicia's encounters with the everyday social performance of beauty and its material effects on her perceptions of her image complicated the construction of a media and critical literacy pedagogy where echoes of global–local power merged with our everyday lives as educators. The teacher presented Alicia's note in the midst of our planning, when Rocío was questioning whether we should continue working on the global discourses of beauty in relation to telenovelas or if we should explore another kind of resource. The teacher, Vivian, who had brought up Alicia's note, first responded to Rocío's ongoing conversation about using telenovelas for the new inquiry cycle and then proceeded to read Alicia's note. She first pointed to the previous explorations of telenovelas and how the problematic beauty discourses in telenovelas emerged in the students' work "cuando exploramos de qué se trataban las novelas y ellos hablaron de que eran bonitas" [when we explored what telenovelas are about and they said that they [women] are beautiful]. At this point, she began to read Alicia's note expressing how Alicia felt rejected by her peers because "soy gorda" [I'm fat], how she perceived this rejection when other children called her "lechona" [a hog], and her struggle to "defenderme" [defend myself]. This hybridized utterance brought visibility to the ways in which two worlds (global media and localized student identity) functioned and merged in our curricular conversation.

Bringing Alicia's personal story to the planning and reflective process opened up another set of parameters to think about the global media inquiry project with the children. Rocío shifted from a curricular direction dilemma, telenovelas or not, into a discussion of our role as facilitators of Alicia's emotional and identity issue: "Lo que a mi me preocuparía de esto es que no se tranforme en algo como a bregar con nuestros issues internos porque yo creo que ninguna de nosotras está preparada." [What concerns me about this is that it doesn't turn into something like how to deal with our inner issues because none of us is prepared to work with inner issues.] Our performed identities shifted from curricular designers/teachers to witness/designers/teachers of the impact of everyday localized oppressive gender social discourses in children's lives. The question that emerged for us was: What should we do about Alicia's experience in relation to our curricular work on global media and critical literacy? The conversation turned into one about understanding the relationship between identity, discourse, and global–local power: "Lo que hay que ver es por qué nosotros tenemos estos issues internos. Porque cuando tú entiendes: 'No soy yo verdad es esto que está allá afuera.' Que si yo tan solo veo mujeres flacas entonces por eso es que me siento como me siento y eso es lo que está mal, no yo." [What we have to see is why do we have those internal issues. Because when you understand: 'It is not me, right? It's what is out there.' Like if I only see women who are skinny then that's why I feel the way I feel and that's what wrong and not me.] For Rocío, Alicia's note produced a context to redefine our work from what media content we should use to how and what outside social power forces (multiple echoes of power, including media) affect the ways that we as women perceive ourselves and are perceived by others. The telenovelas were then brought into the conversation not as curricular texts but as a set of powerful identity texts (Wohlwend, 2009a) that could serve in mediating our understanding of how local female identity discourses are produced with some level of distance: "lo de las novelas crea esa distancia" [the telenovelas create a certain distance].

What happened in this interaction is evidence of how echoes of beauty identity discourses circulate at the global and local levels and how those dynamics moved to the center of our planning work and our future imagined inquiry in the classroom. Nevertheless, the focus on this curriculum design interaction was on the note, the girl as victim, and in Rocío's question. To change the nexus required further inquiry in order to not just change her self-perception but to work with the entire class to change peer culture. Analyzing this interaction, we see the beginning of a rupture to redefine media and literacy work in relation to critical practices on globalization, but we also see much potential for further explorations that open up questions related to a the larger issues of peer culture, identity, and dominant global discourses.

5 Cultural Production of Disney Princess Play Worlds

Karen E. Wohlwend

CULTURAL PRODUCTION IN CLASSROOM PLAY WORLDS

In the Iowa kindergartens where Karen taught and conducted doctoral research, teachers worked to implement permeable curricula (Dyson, 1993) that allowed children to selectively choose material from their popular culture repertoire for play themes and writing projects (Dyson, 2003). When teachers invite transmedia into classroom curricula, the "potent fictions" (Hilton, 1996) of popular culture narratives become available as literacy resources for children to use in classroom play and writing—and as symbolic and cultural capital that children can wield in their power relations with peers (Dyson, 2003; Paley, 1986; Wohlwend, 2011). When children engaged transmedia at school, they negotiated multiple identity texts in addition to curricular expectations for storytelling practices and student dispositions set by school policy and the social histories of who plays with whom constructed in peer culture. Teachers also worked around issues of engaging popular media through play-based literacy curricula, particularly difficult during a decade of intense teacher scrutiny and accountability. Research in these classrooms affords opportunities to see how teachers, children, and their families negotiate complex scripts when adults are simultaneously trying to bring in and keep out popular culture in order to engage but also protect children from perceived media effects.

In the classroom described in this chapter, the kindergarten teacher incorporated children's passion for popular media into writing workshop activities, enabling children to replay engrained gender scripts and to appropriate and revise media characters but also identities for fans and players. Emily, the kindergarten teacher in this classroom, provided a play-based literacy curriculum that incorporated children's media interests as she worked to establish an atmosphere of mutual respect and learner independence. Emily had 17 years of early childhood teaching experience and a master's degree in developmental reading. She was committed to providing an "accepting, peaceful" atmosphere where children could actively participate and feel "comfortable and safe." In a typical morning meeting, Emily welcomed the class, explained her planned activities, and adjusted the day's agenda displayed on a large pocket chart to include activities that children suggested. These plans structured the day into segments: first, shared reading of big books and poetry charts followed by three consecutive 45-minute activity periods that mingled play and children's self-directed reading, writing, and drawing projects.

Karen documented the kinds of popular transmedia in this classroom, marked by SpongeBob, Disney Princess, Spider-Man, and Power Rangers characters that children wore on T-shirts, parkas, mittens, and sneakers and toted to school on backpacks, rest-time towels, lunchboxes, snack foods, folders, markers, erasers, and rulers. Additionally, children brought their own toys, such as Disney Princess dolls and doll-like puppets. Children used transmedia like this to connect with other children as they formed *affinity groups* based on their common play interests and their favorite toys (Fernie, Kantor, & Whaley, 1995). Playgroups were fluid with children joining and leaving throughout the morning as they followed their interests. However, some affinity groups were fairly stable; the children's shared transmedia provided anchors that children could use to return to restart prior play scenarios and reconnect with the same children consistently throughout the year (Wohlwend, 2011). One such group was an affinity group of Disney Princess fans. When these kindergartners wrote, drew, and played with princess transmedia, they strategically emphasized various layered meanings in the animated texts to improvise on prominent gender and transnational identity texts to reshape their participation in classroom cultures.

Classroom cultures are not encapsulated within the walls of a school. Peer cultures and school cultures are always glocalized, specific to a site and simultaneously located in flows such as markets, ideologies, institutional systems, and family and community cultural networks. Some children, such as several girls who were children of international university students, did not recognize popular media characters, could not follow the play themes with these narratives, and could not display or share transmedia markers of membership. Because of this, some children had more difficulty accessing dominant playgroups and less cultural capital in this peer culture (for an account of tensions and affordances around children's transnational imaginaries in this classroom, see Wohlwend & Medina, 2013).

In this chapter, Karen focuses on cultural production through the Disney Princess play of one group of girls and boys who were avid media fans with transnational connections to China, Russia, and the Philippines. These children made up a Disney Princess affinity group in which they reenacted familiar film scripts and expectations for each princess character, quoting memorized dialogue or singing songs from the films as they talked in character while playing with dolls or using princess accessories. In media-based affinity groups like this one, children's transmedia performances cemented their friendships, social practices, cultural knowledges, and peer culture, making rich sites for studying cultural production in overlapping imaginaries.

All the children in the Disney Princess playgroup had transnational family connections: Lily's and Jenna's mothers grew up in China, Stephen and Sasha's grandparents were living in Russia, and Celeste's family planned to return to the Philippines following the completion of her parents' studies at a local university.[1] Close analysis of classroom excerpts among the children provide an in-depth view of the varied and complicated ways that the children inscribed, reinscribed, and revised contradictory cultural scripts. For example, Lily, like the other children in this class, was 5 years old at the beginning of the school year. As she liked to remind her peers, she was born in the year of the dragon (i.e., 2000, as were many children in this classroom). According to her mother, Lily was "American-born Chinese," a child growing up in the U.S. whose parent had grown up in China. In conversations with Lily's teacher, Emily, and in interviews with Karen, Lily's mother expressed hope that her daughter would appreciate Chinese cultural traditions and values. She bemoaned the "lack of respect" that students in American schools exhibited at school in contrast to her own experiences in Chinese schools. In her view, an important potential benefit of Lily's weekend extracurricular classes in Chinese language and literacy was the possibility that Lily might learn more demure ways of responding to adults. However, Lily was a lively child with a wealth of ideas for dramatic play, a talent for leading others, and a passion for Disney Princesses. She toted princess dolls and stuffed toys to school in her backpack and pulled these out during class literacy and play periods. In her play and writing about princesses, she twisted the confining traditional fairy-tale storylines in order to enact more powerful and satisfying roles (Wohlwend, 2009a, 2011).

Similarly, Jenna's parents wanted her to value and learn about her Chinese heritage. Her two mothers shared her adoption story with the class and the ways the couple celebrates Jenna's birthday as the day she arrived in the U.S. when she was a toddler. One of her mothers emigrated from China with her parents and Jenna's grandparents were teaching her to speak and write in Chinese. When she wasn't playing princesses with this playgroup, Jenna could often be found practicing Chinese calligraphy and folding Japanese origami with another girl from China who also attended the Saturday Chinese school with Jenna and Lily.

By contrast, other children in this playgroup did not actively refer to their transnational connections and cultural resources. Stephen and Sasha only occasionally talked about their grandparents in Russia but grew quite excited when a visiting university student spoke a few words in Russian. Celeste, a friendly but also very quiet English-language learner, rarely spoke of her extended family in the Philippines.

As these children played together in and out of imaginary Disney kingdoms, the princess ideal traveled along, intersecting with other scripts circulating through children's families and communities in ways that contradicted and/or resonated with media scripts. The mapping of the network of multiple sites and circulations of Disney Princess transmedia in Figure 3.2 in Chapter 3 shows the pervasive spread of princess products that offer pivots that children easily use to bridge realities in classroom play. Play allowed children to imagine play worlds where boys could be princesses or where *mother* could be plural, stretching normative expectations for performances of gender through scripting: imagining as-if places and laminating media narratives onto histories of identities, practices, and experiences in lived classroom events. To understand how media fueled children's imaginings, the chapter is organized by the same three questions on critical cultural production that framed the inquiry on telenovelas in the previous chapter.

NEGOTIATING PRACTICES FOR PARTICIPATION

How did children collaborate (e.g., negotiate, coordinate roles, interact) to recontextualize sites and access additional nexus of practice:

- Through practices (e.g., song and character enactment) that recontextualized here-and-now cultural spaces?
- Through negotiations and boundary work over who can be an appropriate fan of Disney Princess transmedia?

In this kindergarten, children usually chose where they sat and where they played, creating opportunities to maintain and control their own social groups. Justin, Gavin, Tim, and three other boys often chose to sit and play together, a sports fan affinity group. They created a cohesive and exclusive boys-only space in the classroom by evaluating each other's drawing prowess ("He's a good drawer, you know?"), teaching each other new skills, such as paper airplane folding, collaboratively writing or drawing signs on each other's papers, and engaging in friendly rankings of their favorite sports teams. In the following example (for a full transcript of this vignette, see Appendix A), two members of the sports fans affinity group, Justin and Gavin, sat at the snack table with two Disney Princess players—Stephen and Sasha—and Callie, who played across multiple play groups. Callie, whose family had lived in Iowa for generations like most of the children in this classroom, had no transnational histories and her firsthand experiences and connections to places and people outside the U.S.—or even the state—were framed by special occasions or family vacations.

The five children munched on raisins and Fruit Roll-Ups as they took a break during "choice time," the 45-minute play period at the end of the morning. Children came to the table when they wanted and left when they were finished eating, sometimes returning to a previous center to resume their play activity and sometimes following a friend to a new play activity. This made the snack area a transitional space where children fluidly switched playgroups and a good place to recruit friends for play activities around shared interests in popular media. In the following inter-action, the five children positioned each other in what appears to be a performative competition between Justin as rap music fan and Sasha and Stephen as Disney Princess fans as the three boys try to attract Gavin's or Callie's interest to Justin's new CD collection or Stephen's rendition of a song from an *Aladdin* direct-to-DVD sequel.

In this section, seven excerpts present the entire episode where Sasha and Stephen ruptured identity texts that indexed implicit branding prac-tices that targeted girls as *the* (only) appropriate consumers and fans for Disney Princess films. In this competitive exchange, Stephen and Sasha's shared knowledge of lyrics from the wedding song in the *Aladdin* direct-to-video sequel *Aladdin and the King of Thieves* was pitted against Jus-tin's references to ownership of 16 or more rap CDs *and* the Aladdin video. To establish their relative status in the peer culture, Stephen and Sasha used their knowledge and performance of songs to position them-selves as Disney Princess experts; by contrast, Justin signaled his physical possession of songs and CDs as material capital to position himself as a collector of valued multimedia.

Initially, Gavin shared Stephen and Sasha's interest in the Disney Prin-cess film and joined them in singing the song. Justin directly responded only once to Stephen's comments, and then it was to challenge his pronunciation of *Africa*. Justin used multiple modal resources to distance himself from the Disney Princess play: turning his back, averting his gaze, distracting Gavin with a new topic, and increasing his proximity to Gavin by leaning across the table. Meanwhile, Stephen and Sasha demonstrated their inter-est as fans by spending several turns working out the correct pronuncia-tion of Agrabah, the fictional kingdom in *Aladdin*. In this example, Gavin acknowledged that he knew the Aladdin song and established a social con-nection with Stephen and Sasha.

Vignette 1

Aladdin Excerpt 1:

Stephen: There's a song about [*singing*] "There's a party here in Africa."
         [*waving one hand with raisin above his head in a circling motion*]
Gavin: I know.
Stephen: You heard, uh, you watched it! *Aladdin, King of Thieves?*
Gavin: Yeah.
Stephen: That's me too! I watched it at my grandma's.
Sasha: What about—did you watch—about in Abraguuh
Stephen: Well, we did. At my grandma's.
Sasha: What about Aladdin of Jasmine?

Unlike Gavin, Justin ignored Stephen's overture, "Did you watch, umm, *Aladdin, King of Thieves*? There's a song about [*singing*] 'There's a party here in Africa,'" responding with a correction that begins a sequence on competing opinions on the proper pronunciation of the word Agrabah.

Aladdin Excerpt 2:

Stephen: [to Justin] Did you watch, umm, *Aladdin, King of Thieves*? There's a song about [*singing*] "There's a party here in Africa."
Justin: No, Africa's not.
Stephen: [*disagreeing with Justin*] I hearrd.
Gavin: [*agreeing with Stephen*] And me. Okay, this is slippery. [*trying to open box of raisins*]
Justin: [to Gavin] Hey, guess what?
Gavin: [*singing*] "There's a party here in Africa."
Sasha: Abriga
Stephen: [*noticing his own error in pronunciation*] ABRIGah, not Africa. Abrigah.
Sasha: [*to Stephen, correcting his pronunciation*] AbregUH, GUH
Stephen: Abriguh, Abriguh
Sasha: [*nods head to approve pronunciation*]

Justin began a second competition and attempted to turn Gavin's attention away from the Disney Princess song. Nexus analysis reveals textual layers in this moment of negotiation in a verbal contest between Stephen, Sasha, and Justin that pits a Disney Princess song against claims about ownership of a set of rap CDs. Justin quickly turned the conversation away from Sasha and Stephen's singing of a Disney Princess song to highlight the quantity of his own music collection. His pivot to competition enacted an identity as an *individual competitor*, consistent with hierarchical values that are situated in a discourse of hegemonic masculinity that promotes a need for rankings to establish dominant individuals (Blaise, 2005): "In the kindergarten classroom, hegemonic masculinity can be thought of as the most desirable and powerful way to be a boy" (p. 21). Justin, Gavin, and other boys in their sports affinity group rarely engaged in doll play, preferring to draw or write about sports themes strongly linked to a masculinity associated with sports and competition (Connell & Messerschmidt, 2005; Kane, 2003). Their group's social dominance in sports on the playground enabled them to organize games, determine rules, and select members of their teams. This dominance spilled over into the classroom peer culture as boys competed through sports talk that displayed their team knowledge and enacted a male identity text of an avid football fan (Whannel, 2001) that circulated widely in this rural Midwestern state. When Justin failed to get Gavin's attention—"Hey, guess what?"—he began talking to Callie repeatedly about his "CD pack."

Aladdin Excerpt 3:

Justin: [to Callie across the table] I have a whole CD pack at home. A whole CD pack. [*adding emphasis with a wave of his arm*] A whole CD pack. Can you believe that?
Callie: No wonder.

When Stephen focused his attention on Callie, Justin tried to engage Gavin and perhaps impress him with talk about new birthday presents, emphasizing that his new "whole CD pack" was "not Aladdin" and implicitly rejecting Stephen's situated identity as a Disney Princess fan. Justin underscored this rejection by bodily turning away from Stephen. Justin stressed the word "wap" (probably his approximation of "rap," making it a marker of adolescent taste and superior status) by saying it louder and repeating it.

Aladdin Excerpt 4:

Stephen: [to Callie] Callie, did you watch *Aladdin, King of Thieves*? There's a song about [*singing*] "There's a party here in Afriguh. We all know can't wait."
Justin: [*leaning across table to address Gavin*] Hey, guess what? I have a whole CD pack at home. A whole CD pack. Can you believe that? A whole CD pack. But not Aladdin [*turning away from Stephen*] CD. It's wap [*louder*].
Justin: [*after no response from Gavin, repeats*] It's wap.

Justin shifted his focus to Callie when she expressed a deferential interest by echoing his comments and by asking how many CDs he owned.

Aladdin Excerpt 5:

Callie: [to Justin] How many do you have?
Sasha: [*singing*] We almost can't wait. There's a party here in Abrigah.
Justin: [to Callie] 19. 19. Like 19. I have 19.
Callie: [to Justin] Well I have that other one.
Justin: [to Callie] I have, I like have, I have 16. I have like 16 CDs. I even got a pack for my birthday. I got two CDs for my birthday and a radio. And a holder. For my birthday.
Callie: He got two.
Justin: I got all of that for my birthday. Can you believe it? And fish. Two fish.

Callie's responses aligned with an admiring follower identity consistent with an emphasized femininity expressed through the Disney Princess films in which girls and women appreciatively reflect and amplify male accomplishments

(Blaise, 2005; Connell & Messerschmidt, 2005; Hilton, 1996). Discourses are relational so that the deferent femininity enacted by Callie is positioned as subordinate to the hegemonic masculinity enacted by Justin. When Callie attempted to enter the competition and also enact an individual competitor identity with a claim that she had "that other one," Justin ignored her claim. Instead, he immediately elaborated with a repeated count—"19. 19. Like 19. I have 19"—to back up his claim that he had a whole pack of CDs, followed by a litany of additional birthday presents.

All the while, Sasha was singing, repeating the first line and inventing a second line for the wedding party song, "There's a party here in Abrigah. We almost can't wait. There's a party here in Abrigah." Stephen attempted to enter into the CD competition, "I got a hundred of 'em," a repeated claim that went unacknowledged by other children at the table. Callie turned back to Justin and reverted to her encouraging subordinate role, urging him to continue and, implicitly to ignore Stephen's interruption, to "keep talkin'." Justin reinforced his situated identity owner by stressing his right and ability to carry out a literacy practice that marked his sole ownership of this material capital: "I writed my name all over it."

Aladdin Excerpt 6:

Justin: I got all of that for my birthday. Can you believe it? And fish. Two fish.
Stephen: I got a hundred of 'em.
Justin: No. Really. REALLY. I got fish for my birthday and a radio and two CDs and a holder for 'em.
Stephen: [*simultaneously*] A hundred of 'em.
Callie: [to Justin] Keep talkin' keep talkin' keep talkin'.
Justin: I had my name all over it. I writed my name all over it.
Stephen: A hundred of 'em.

This example demonstrates the disparate power relations between a dominant masculinity circulating among kindergarten boys in one playgroup, a femininity voiced by Callie, and a nondominant masculinity performed by Stephen and Sasha. Callie's questions to Justin and her inattention to Stephen tended to marginalize Sasha and Stephen's media knowledge of Disney Princess fans. Although she also played Disney Princess themes in the dollhouse with these boys, she ignored Stephen's talk about the Aladdin film and did not take up a Disney Princess fan identity in this exchange. Later, Stephen played out a bit of the film:

Aladdin Excerpt 7:

Stephen: [*stands up to enact a pose as Jafar the villain from* Aladdin]
Justin: I HAVE Aladdin.

Stephen: You don't have *Aladdin Jafar Part II.*

Justin: [*looks at Callie, blinking in an exaggerated way while slapping his own head repeatedly—a move reminiscent of Three Stooges slapstick*]

Justin's comic action diverted the group's attention away from the competition between Stephen and Sasha's symbolic capital in the form of script knowledge and Justin's material capital in the claim of 16 CDs and two fish. In peer interactions through the school year, Justin's play activities remained markedly separate from those of Sasha, Stephen, and the other Disney Princess players. However, Gavin and Tim continued to join in princess play scenarios from time to time as well as boys and girls from other playgroups.

EMBODYING MEDIA IDENTITY TEXTS AND IMPROVISING TO EXPAND THE NEXUS OF FAMILY

During classroom play scenarios at the dollhouse or in the housekeeping corner, children embodied character identity texts, through performances that enacted a character in live-action plays or animated a doll as a proxy for oneself. Negotiations of character roles and storylines were a key element of Disney Princess pretend play as children rationed out fairy-tale roles to interested players. Joining a playgroup in progress caused further complications as children needed to make room: physically by sharing dolls and materials and socially according to class friendships, but also semiotically as character roles needed to be attached to dolls and players in ways that made sense for the story. Children drew upon their knowledge of family structures to script fantasy families that fit their playgroup needs and their literacy knowledge of sensible storylines.

❅ ❅

Vignette 2: Negotiating Gender and Scripting Family

Sasha, Lily, Celeste, and Stephen are standing in front of the pink–and–lavender-trimmed plastic dollhouse, set in its usual place on top of the writing table. Sasha hands a small, fist-sized blonde princess doll to Celeste. Celeste, whose friendly acquiescence makes her one of the most popular kindergartners, obliges him by taking the doll but almost immediately sets it aside. She and Lily are busy locating baby furniture for the nursery on the upper floor of the two-story pink-and-white plastic dollhouse. Lily's hands move quickly and decisively to move furniture and dolls from room to room.

Lily: This baby is a girrrl. [*picking up a bald doll with a permanent crouching pose that allows it to just fit into the plastic baby*

swing; she voices a monotonous infant's wail] Waa-waa. Mama.
Waa-waa.

Jenna: [*approaching the periphery of the playgroup*] Can I play with
you guys? Can I please play? Can I be her? [*picks up a doll who
is clad in denim jeans and a red sailor shirt; with Jenna's arrival
comes a need for players to assign, clarify, and justify their
agreed-upon roles and doll identities*]

Lily: You're a boy. [*tacitly accepting Jenna into the play scenario and
framing her participation as animator of a boy character*]

Sasha: I'm Mary Poppins[2], so I'm a girl.

Jenna: [*moves her doll up the side of the dollhouse and bounces it
across the roof; her action is an implicit agreement, accepting
the assigned "boy" identity to quickly join the play*]

Sasha: [*indicating Jenna's doll with short bob, plaid shirt, denim pants
in a clarification that reopens role negotiations*] It means a boy
orrrr a girl.

Stephen: We're a superhero family, okay? And I'm sweeping up on the chimin,
[*singing with an invented tune*] I'm sweeping up on the chimin.

Sasha: [*repeating*] I'm Mary Poppins, so I'm a girl.

Jenna: [*moves her doll up the side of the dollhouse and bounces it across
the roof*]

Sasha: [*indicating Jenna's doll again and continuing to keep the doll's gender unfixed*] It (xx) a boy or a girl or—so it means a boy or a girl.

Jenna: [*improvising, moves her doll to the baby swing, offering to run
the baby swing, which suggests a changed role, from child to
adult*] Who wants to go swinging?

Stephen: [*recognizing Jenna's doll in new role and switching doll's gender
through further improvisation*] Mommy, Mommy! I'm going to
go swimming!

Jenna: [*holding her doll in front of her face to have the now-mother (boy/
girl doll) correct her child (Stephen's tiny woman doll)*] No, swing.
[*takes Stephen's doll out of his hand to put it in the baby swing*]

Stephen: [*objecting*] Whyyyy, Mom? I can fly!

In the kindergarten housekeeping center, play negotiations over who would
play which roles created opportunities to rescript gender roles, particularly
when multiple players wanted to embody the same desirable role or character identity. In these cases, children improvised, proliferating roles by
adding additional mothers, fairies, or princesses, switching the gender of
particular dolls, or multiplying the number of mothers, sisters, brothers. In
these negotiations, identity texts and gender expectations within the nexus
of practice of *family* were made visible but also malleable. In the following
example, children explored the cultural tensions around the family feminine identities *mommy, stepmother, grandma,* and *mom* as they wielded
the implicit power relationships signified by these kinship terms to negotiate who would—and who would not—play the central role of mother.

Vignette 3: Negotiating Mother

"Ding-dong." Intoning the falling two-tone pitch of a doorbell, Celeste stands in a child-size gap between the light blue refrigerator and the white wooden cupboard that define one wall of the housekeeping center. No one responds, so she repeats her doorbell insistently:

Celeste:	Ding-dong-ding-dong-ding-dong.
Stephen:	[*in a shiny red plastic fire hat and an adult's turquoise T-shirt that droops past his knees, rushes to the "door"*] Oh, Grandma's here.
Celeste:	No, I'm the mommy.
Stephen:	No, you're our stepmother.
Erin:	[*turning away from the small wooden kitchen table to echo Stephen's objection*] No, you're the grandma 'cause I'm the mom. [*she chews convincingly on a plastic carrot*]
Stephen:	[*agreeing with Erin*] We already traded. And I'm the red star winner, so I get the star. And we all can save the day. We're superheroes too.

✻ ✻

In this example, children renegotiated roles and improvised family structures through a break in the pretense, stepping outside the play frame to explicitly explain and justify roles. "We already traded" signals that the roles, while pretend, had been determined by consensus and were already fixed. Furthermore, Stephen used this opening to not only improvise another role but to position himself as a special superhero with an imagined red star, through the added improvisation of a superhero family. This improvisation opened more possibilities for more play action as a superhero family could now use superpowers such as flying. This opening altered the structure of the play family and allowed alternative scripts to emerge that could include a mother and grandmother, or perhaps a stepmother inspired by a Disney Princess villain. Creating superpowered families was a common trope in children's Disney Princess play that also opened up possibilities for more players as it connected Stephen and Sasha's interest in Disney Princess media with other boys' interest in superhero media like Spider-Man and Power Rangers.

SCRIPTING AND RESCRIPTING MEDIA NARRATIVES

Play that ruptured the commercial narratives altered storylines and enabled new roles to emerge that attracted a wider range of players, including boys who could be persuaded to play Cinderella's brothers or fairy godmothers if they could also have superpowers. During play, Stephen and Sasha draped aprons over their heads and would flip their "hair" in roles as Ariel the Little Mermaid or Jasmine. They used dolls to enact other Disney Princesses (especially Snow White, Sleeping Beauty, or Cinderella) or powerful villains (the evil Queen from *Snow White and the Seven Dwarfs* or Ursula the Sea Witch from

The Little Mermaid). They also improvised to give superpowers and fighting abilities to Cinderella's Fairy Godmother as in the following example.

Vignette 4: Rescripting Cinderella

Stephen: She's the Fairy Godmother! [*holding up a tiny molded plastic woman as he waves his arms as if brandishing a wand in large circles*] You know Fairy Godmother?
Callie: Cinderella?
Stephen: No! Cinderella is different than Fairy Godmother!
Sasha: Yes, a witch! [*holding a princess doll*]

Later, Darnell approaches the dollhouse where Stephen, Sasha, and Gavin are continuing the "Fairy Godmother" play theme: Stephen's tiny dollhouse mother doll is Cinderella's Fairy Godmother, Sasha is animating the princess doll as a "Scary Godmother," a witch version of the kindly fairy godmother from the Cinderella film, and Gavin is fighting both godmothers with the miniature baby doll.

Darnell: Can I play?
Stephen: We're playing Fairy Godmother.
Darnell: [*picks up the boy/girl doll in the plaid shirt and places it in the dollhouse*]
Stephen: [*flies the fairy godmother doll in circles and lands it on the dollhouse roof*]
Darnell: Daddy, you're home! I'm glad you're not killed.
Stephen: [*to Darnell, negotiating Darnell's doll's role*] He's not my son; he's my cousin.
Gavin: [*voicing the baby character*] Mommy tells me every day to tell you what to do.
Darnell: Can I be the brother?
Sasha: No, Michael's the baby. [*indicating Gavin's crouching baby doll whom they have named Michael*]
Darnell: What are you guys going to name me?
Sasha: Cinderella.
Darnell: [*protesting*] But I want to be the brother.
Sasha: That IS the brother.

With character roles established, play resumes with rough-and-tumble play in which the boys take turns knocking the brother dolls off the top of the dollhouse as the Fairy Godmother and brothers fight off Sasha's "Scary Godmother." The play ends with various dolls swooshing around the dollhouse in flying baby cribs and intermittently docking with the "spaceship," which is the teacher's computer-turned-mother-ship.

This vignette shows that the identity texts that children write and rewrite are also inscribed on bodies and not limited to a single media narrative identity text, but merge multiple scripts. For example, particular identity texts or ways of being at school are inscribed on children's bodies when they are taught to write and act at school in particular ways: raising hands for a turn to speak, holding a pencil just so. Everyday identity texts are scripted and rescripted through similar embodied actions that are frequently not produced in a durable form. A writing workshop script in Emily's kindergarten classroom legitimated child-directed writing practices and author identities, positioning children as creative authors who could import Disney Princess media as literary resources and print to create their own original scripts or, more typically, variations on the commercial fairy tales.

Jenna and Lily also regularly wrote and played with Stephen and Sasha to enact Disney Princess narratives. Frequently, the children drew pictures and wrote captions to create short books, puppet show scripts, and plays about princess characters. When Jenna and Lily played with and wrote about Disney Princess dolls, they reproduced (and sometimes contested) prevalent gender stereotypes in commercial media and in toy manufacturer's expectations for typical toy users. Disney Princess dolls and texts provided opportunities to play anticipated identities associated with discourses of emphasized femininity that the girls found simultaneously appealing and confining. Disney Princess media drew from and reinscribed Whiteness beauty ideals and norms for hyperfeminine performances (Baker-Sperrey & Grauerholz, 2003; Hurley, 2005; Lee, 2006). The Disney Princess storylines teach girls the importance of being desired and being loved. When romantic love comes to school, as it does through the princess media, children create their own ways of negotiating these texts. As Madrid (2011) shows, preschool children have their own way of making sense of romantic love, by reframing the notions of boyfriends, girlfriends, and sexual and family relationships as they work at imagining gendered worlds into being among themselves in peer culture.

Disney Princess commercial scripts and families' expectations converged in complicated ways in children's performances as girls, daughters, and princesses. It is likely that Jenna and Lily experienced and negotiated layers of cross-cultural tensions as Chinese American girls playing American versions of primarily White heroines in Western fairy tales. Across the transmedia merchandise, princess characters dress like European royalty and live in medieval castles. Regardless of their ethnicities or Old World trappings, in animated films and multimedia, Disney Princesses talk and act like middle-class American teenagers.

Rescripting the Disney Princess Family

When Jenna played Disney Princesses, she took up the princess scripts and their heteronormative nexus of practice for family configurations. For example, the imperative to marry and the obligatory (heterosexual) wedding necessary for a happily-ever-after are consistent with the goals of the hyperfeminine scripts (Walkerdine, 1984). Another recurring trope in Disney scripts is the necessity for the heroine to find or create a "good family," particularly in the abused stepdaughter to princess-bride storylines in *Cinderella* and *Snow White*. Although heterosexual marriage is the tacit ideal in this nexus, the most common family structure scripted across the 13 films is the one-parent family. This creates dramatic tension in the films as a ruptured ideal that positions the Disney Princess as alone against the world. Disney Princesses tend to be only children (see Table 5.1). A key element is loss of family through deceased or absent biological parents while adoptive parents (i.e., stepmothers) are portrayed as cruel and scheming villains making nonbiological family relations suspect in Disney's representations of family. An exception is the temporary family created when three benevolent and grandmotherly fairies sneak Sleeping Beauty into hiding to protect her from the evil Maleficent (an animated version of a witness protection program); this creates an alternative family structure in which three women raise Sleeping Beauty from birth to adolescence.

Table 5.1   Family Roles and Relationships in Disney Princess Films

Princess	Father	Mother	Stepmother	Grandmothers or Surrogate Grandmothers	Siblings
Snow White	Deceased	Deceased	Queen, stepmother		
Cinderella	Deceased	Deceased	Lady Tremaine, stepmother	Fairy Godmother	Two stepsisters
Ariel	King Triton	Queen Athena, deceased			Six sisters
Belle	Maurice	Deceased/ absent			
Jasmine	The Sultan	Deceased/ absent			
Pocahontas	Chief Powhatan	Deceased			
Aurora	King Stephan, backgrounded	Queen Leah, back- grounded		Flora, Fauna, and Merriweather; fairies as tempo- rary parents	
Mulan	Fa Zhou	Fa Li		Grandmother Fa	
Tiana	James, deceased	Eudora			
Rapunzel	King Thomas, backgrounded	Queen Primrose, back- grounded	Mother Gothel, step- mother by kidnapping		
Merida	King Fergus	Queen Elinor			Three brothers (triplets)
Anna and Elsa (sisters)	Deceased	Deceased			

Expanding the "Good Family" in Disney Princess Media

Jenna's early versions of a Disney Princess–inspired fairy tale began with a storyboard and stick puppets that reflected an idealized heterosexual nuclear family: a king, a queen, a princess, and a prince (Figures 5.1 and 5.2).

Jenna's narration of her storyboard:

1. They're walking up the stairs.
2. When they are, and this is the—that they're going here.
3. When they see a princess's grandmother.
4. When they're laying down in their bed.
5. And this is when they came down the stairs.
6. And this is when they go out into there.
7. When they're drinking hot cocoa and making it here.
8. Drinking it.

Over the course of several weeks, she added a script and created a castle backdrop and related props, such as paper cocoa mugs taped to popsicle sticks in Figure 5.2.

Figure 5.1 Jenna's storyboard.

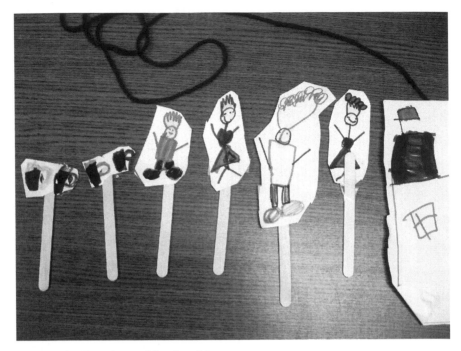

Figure 5.2 Jenna's royal family stick puppets.

After playing the story over the course of several weeks, she revised rewrote her script to shift the characters and the heterosexual norms attached to her stick puppets.

Jenna's Written Script for Her Puppet Show

"There's 2 kings, 1 queen, and 1 princess. I finished this all yesterday, the whole page." Large letters fill each page:

LIS GO UPSARS	[Princess:] Let's go upstairs
to See MY GAMA	to see my grandma.
Th WAK	They walk
UPsTARS	upstairs.
the qweN AND KeN WAt!	The queen and king went
INtO the KASL!	into the castle
ANd tuc A NAP.	and took a nap

Gender scripts in play worlds are influenced by identity texts that shape how children understand *family*, at home and at school (Ryan, 2010) as well as in fictional media worlds. Emily worked in this classroom to value diversity in representations of families in trade books and children's writing. Even so, school scripts in newsletters, policies, and designs for special events upheld heterosexual nexus and Jenna's family approached Emily for support when tacit heteronormative school expectations seemed to require a different family structure. For example, Jenna's mothers were concerned about a school-sponsored activity—"Dad's Night"—where children were to come with their fathers and engage in a fair with a "masculine" theme: three-legged races, basketball contests, and other sports-related activities. Jenna's mothers asked Emily, "Do we have to come up with a dad for Dad's Night?" and Emily quickly reassured them that this was of course not necessary. But later when Emily shared this with Karen, she expressed chagrin that a school-sanctioned event had positioned Jenna's family as somehow lacking.

Scripting Mulan

Crisp winter sunshine fills the kindergarten classroom. At each table, clusters of children chatter as they draw birthday cards for Min, who is quietly drawing six-corner stars in her journal. Jenna stops drawing and walks around the table to peer intently into Min's face. "Can I see the color of your eyes?" As if satisfying a hunch, Jenna pronounces "brown" and walks back to color brown eyes on her birthday card. Across the table, Lily is filling a card with neon-colored tigers while talking about her own birthday, which is a few months away. Lily announces, to no one in particular, "Whoever is born under a dragon is special. My mother says."

Five-year-old Lily drew upon her knowledge of symbols of a Chinese calendar to imply that *she* is the one who is special. However, several children in this kindergarten shared the same birth year as well as transnational connections to China. Jenna and Lily's shared connections to China, and their interest in Chinese language, literacy, and culture created a bond that shaped their play and classroom friendships as they collectively engaged imagined worlds that caused them to negotiate identity texts circulating across scapes of family life, school, and children's popular media.

Lily's family encouraged her to play with Mulan, the Chinese heroine of a historical epic that Disney appropriated for its princess franchise. In the Chinese historical text, Mulan is a dutiful daughter who masquerades as a boy to fulfill her family's obligation to send someone to serve in the emperor's army. In the Disney version, Mulan is rewritten from a revered warrior to a young girl as much concerned with winning the affection of the hero as she is in upholding her family's honor. Furthermore, Disney Mulan's strength is positioned as highly unusual for a girl.

> The character of Mulan is neither seductive or voluptuous; she is probably the only Disney heroine who is emotionally and physically strong and does not wait around for Prince Charming to save her. In order to put Mulan on a pedestal, however, Disney stomps on the people and culture around her. The China of Mulan is the most oppressive, rigid, and sexist culture in the world of Disney's animated children's movies. (Sun, 2011, p. 108)

In the film, musical montages such as "I'll Make a Man out of You" repeat the message that gender is an obstacle to be overcome, that Mulan becomes a hero in spite of her culture and gender: as Mulan's wise-cracking sidekick Mushu reminds her, "People don't listen—you're a girl again, remember?" The final scenes emphasize that a happy ending depends upon a successful culmination of the film's romantic plot: marriage with her former squad leader, Li Shang, the handsome son of a general. This aligns with a common theme in Disney Princess romantic scripts that end with heroines winning the affection of princely heroes. In Disney's description of the DVD, Mulan is "clever"—her "adventures lead to a climactic battle" that saves China—but it is Chang, an invented hero added by Disney, who is described as "courageous." Even a cursory deconstruction of the passage shows that Mulan is not an active subject here; rather her adventures somewhat ambiguously produce a climactic battle as Disney rhetorically distances this princess from fighting and winning the battle.

> Clever Mulan proves her worth outside of her tradition-bound society when, disguised as a male soldier, "Ping," she bravely takes her father's place in the Imperial Army. Helped by her outrageously funny guardian dragon Mushu and a lucky cricket named Cri-Kee, Mulan strives to earn the respect of her fellow warriors and their courageous Captain Shang. Mulan's adventures lead to a climactic battle atop the Imperial Palace, where her family's honor and the fate of the Emperor and all of China rests in her hands! (Disney DVD, 2011)

Nevertheless, Lily's mother believed that Mulan introduced an Asian beauty ideal in the princess franchise and provided an ostensibly less passive role model than the other Disney Princess identity texts. It is important to note that the initial film narrative is only one part of the Mulan script; Disney transmedia included Mulan direct-to-video sequels, imagined and crafted by Disney writers, with storylines that diverge even more from the original tale of a honored female warrior.

❋ ❋

Vignette 5: Scripting Mulan and Scripting Family

Lily quickly sketches on her paper, which will become pages of her book. Across the table, two boys, Sasha and Conor, are drawing pictures of their own. Sasha and Lily are writing stories about Mulan, the title character in the Disney Princess film set in China.

Sasha: [*leans across the table and inspects her drawing*] How about the three princesses?

Lily: There aren't three princesses.

Sasha: In *Mulan II*! She has three friends and they are the three princesses.

Lily: I only know Mulan. [*resumes drawing*]

Sasha: This is Mulan [*indicating his drawing*] here a long time ago before she got married. That was just Mulan, *Mulan I*. Well, she has black hair. It was on *Mulan II* but she has black hair.

Lily: All I remember from the movie is Mulan.

Sasha: How 'bout the three princesses?

Lily: There *is* no three princesses!

Sasha: There is!

Lily: In Mulan?

Sasha: Yes! No, in *Mulan II*—

Lily: Is Mulan the three princesses?

Sasha: No, *Mulan I*.

Conor: huuuh [*sighs, exasperated by Sasha and Lily's argument*]

Sasha: In *Mulan II*, she has some three friends, three friends that are *princesses*. And she's, she's one of the *four* princesses. 'Cause there were four of her. Okay, I'm done with this [marker]. Okay, here.

Conor: No, there isn't.

Sasha: Yes, there is. There is on Mu—

Conor: There is not.

Sasha: There is.

Conor: huuh [*sighs*]

Conor: Don't move that, can't move it away.

Lily: This is when Mulan's mom got married. But I don't want those pages.

Conor: HUUH [*sighs loudly*]

Back at the table, Lily shows her journal to Karen and points out that she was working on a "bear story but now I'm doing a Mulan story. This is her mother, this is her friend, and that is her husband. And they're getting married. And this is a doll that she has and this is another doll that she has. The mommy is getting so excited."

※ ※

This episode demonstrates the tensions among the children's depth of attachment to the stories they loved, their desire to make the story their own but also to retell the story correctly in a faithful portrayal. Media is a cultural resource wrapped in longing and belonging (Pugh, 2009) that children use for displaying and wielding cultural resources, reproducing social norms, and participating in playgroups (Wohlwend, 2011) that are localized globals (Santos, 2006). The young children that Karen observed in this kindergarten did not participate directly in the kinds of embodied, online media communities of practice in spoiler communities described by Jenkins (2006) or in fanfiction sites described by Black (2009). Instead, children collectively imagined gendered worlds that operated along the lines of Holland and colleague's conceptualization of (1998) figured worlds—an imaginary that includes a set of scripts that are taken up locally and taken in among children who embody and perform those worlds.

The children's cultural production reproduced, appropriated, and transgressed given models and reframed them into personal productions that adhered to different rules and values. The children's unique negotiation of transnational, media, and gender identity texts was a cultural production that spanned peer and school cultures. This is aesthetic labor—the visual and performative work of making discourse live in the local. Children play what they know and they play to make sense of and participate in the worlds around them. The vignettes in this chapter illustrate the power of providing children with familiar props as resources that allow them to connect with each other. Teachers who engage the nexus of practice in their classrooms and recognize the scripts and discourses in children's' play in peer cultures can work across school cultures and imagined worlds with the goal of helping children connect to each other and to their cultural resources. This requires knowledge of the nexus and materials that children value so that teachers can work with and when necessary against play when it becomes exclusionary. Emily worked to change the nexus in classroom cultures by inviting media into the kindergarten where children could openly negotiate text meanings but also by positioning children as thoughtful and caring players who could alter the roles in texts to include rather than exclude players. She opened participation structures by allowing children to determine the number of players at a center and encouraging children to teach and share their areas of expertise (See also Wohlwend & Medina, 2013).

Even so, the convergences of transnational, media, and gender nexus of practice produced tensions as children took up play texts that conflicted with family cultural values or contradicted peer interpretations of gender roles in film narratives. For example, the characterizations of evil or comical dragons in *Sleeping Beauty* and *Mulan* in the books and film that Lily made conflicted with her family's values and cultural traditions that revered dragons. With the purpose of critically engaging multiple imagined worlds, this analysis of scripting in nexus of practice reveals the ways children negotiate, uphold, and improvise scripts for belonging in transnational cultural repertoires and literacy practices in U.S. schooling and gender expectations, such as in Disney Princess media, circulating across consumer markets and peer cultures.

6 Convergences and Slippages in Children's Improvisations and Teachers' Pedagogical Imaginaries

Throughout the book we have argued and demonstrated how processes of localizing and re-localizing deterritorialized transnational and global discourses are embedded in people's ability to move across landscapes, and to simultaneously negotiate being and becoming participants in multiple worlds and imaginaries. In our view of literacy work as collective cultural production, we see the literacy subject not as reading and/or producing texts in one linear way, in one place, and in isolation; instead, she or he reads and produces texts across landscapes, bringing her or his ability to move across and participate in multiple textual worlds, cultural imaginaries, and habitats of meaning making. However, as we look at our experiences as educators and researchers collaborating with teachers, we also find interesting the ways that negotiations and boundaries are established across teachers' and students' knowledge. While the teachers and researchers make curricular decisions based on their imaginaries of schooling, the students playfully engage in renegotiating their understanding of the multiple worlds that intersect in their classroom work. In these instances, teachers' and researchers' out-of-school knowledge, ways of doing literacy in classrooms, and interpretations of cultural production often clash with those of the children. Blommaert (2008) argues that in the flows of literacies and discourses across locations, meanings are lost, recontextualized, and misunderstood. Similarly, we argue that even when teachers' and researchers' good intentions frame a particular curricular experience as literacy as children's cultural production, adults' perspectives sometimes clash with and get privileged over those of the students. Such clashes are interesting performative moments that provide clarity as to how teacher identities are enacted as impositions—of adult views and of what counts as knowledge—that shape whose knowledge gets legitimized, misunderstood, or marginalized.

However, what we found most compelling was how engaging with out-of-school imaginaries creates ruptures that open up opportunities for other potential conversations and experiences in the classroom between students and teachers. At times, these ruptures caused teachers and researchers to reexamine their teaching or the classroom environment and to reimagine possible ways for children to participate. In the next sections, Carmen shares additional data from her study on telenovelas and Karen shares her work on transmedia play in preschool contexts as we demonstrate how teachers in both contexts negotiated tensions around integrating popular media, literacy, and film-making in their classrooms. We look across these studies to analyze both the clashes and possibilities as teachers, researchers, and students negotiated multiple nexus of practices and cultural imaginaries.

CONVERGENCES AND CLASHES AMONG POPULAR CULTURES AND TEACHER KNOWLEDGE IMAGINARIES

In Carmen's work around the students' production of telenovelas, it was interesting to pay attention to the multiple other recontextualizations across global and local landscapes that the students produced. Once a space was opened in the classroom to deliberately bring, improvise, and play around popular culture imaginaries, the students enacted a sense of agency and empowerment in collectively scripting, creating, and improvising other kinds of texts and identities. Their enactments expanded what we traditionally see in classrooms and created ruptures for new ways of knowing and new ways of doing literacy work to emerge. A shift in the ways the teachers viewed, constructed, and enacted literacy curricula as cultural production fostered a new classroom pedagogy. Although contested at many times, this performative literacy pedagogy repositioned and recentered children's work.

Barrio en la Calle/Barrio on the Streets, a telenovela devised and performed by three boys, was one of these texts produced through a performative approach to literacy. By pushing the boundaries of the telenovela's context into other global imaginaries, the children's telenovela shifted and transformed the teachers' ideas of how knowledge emerges, what ways of knowing become relevant in improvisation, and who holds "the knowledge" in the classroom. The tactical ways in which these three boys approached and improvised around the production of their telenovela reveal many layers of agency in the process of enacting and playing with other cultural resources that add to the complex landscape that was created in this project.

Figure 6.1 *Barrio en la Calle/Barrio on the Streets.*

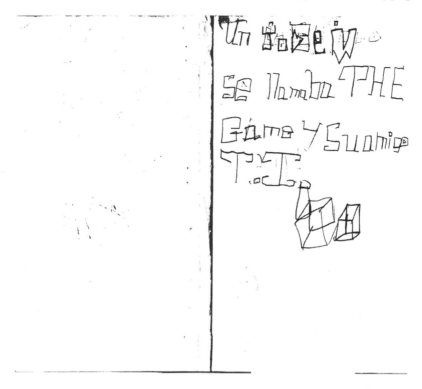

Figure 6.2 The Game and T.I. as protagonists.

In the first draft of their telenovela, the boys tell the story of "The Game" and "T.I." who are friends:

> The Game falls in love with a girl and they get married. The Game invites his wife to take a walk in Old San Juan and during their walk, a thief comes to rob her and take her purse. The Game and T.I. fight with the robbers and eventually the police trap the robber and he returns the purse. Finally, The Game and his wife live happily ever after.

In some ways the traditional elements of a telenovela or story are clearly there. The man falls in love with a woman, there is a conflict, it gets resolved, and they live happily ever after. However, a close look at the details in this telenovela shows that the context the students created to imagine, locate, and produce their ideas is not a simple one. To see its complexity, we must appreciate how the students manipulated multiple cultural references in their mobility across global and local landscapes in their improvisational work localizing multiple globals.

First, consider the choice of title: *Barrio en la Calle* [Barrio on the Streets]. In the same way that a telenovela title such as *Tormenta en el Paraíso* [Storm in Paradise] provides the audience with a spatial context for engaging with the telenovela text, the students used the title to situate the audience through a spatialized reference. The "where" matters; the barrio is lived "on the streets" versus in houses or other possible places in the community. The title provides the context for the story while signifying the importance of space and location to situate the events and in the process of conveying their intentions in the overall composition of the text. *Barrio en la Calle* [Barrio on the Streets], the students shared in their analysis of their text, signifies lives in the streets of a neighborhood and the living in a neighborhood as it is experienced by "gente de la calle" [people from the streets]. They came to the production of this text with knowledge and a history of making sense of particular lifestyles informed by popular culture: specifically hip-hop culture. The children resituated this knowledge by locating the events and characters in San Juan (the capital city of Puerto Rico) and making it work within the genre of a telenovela. Like Blommaert's accounts on texts that do not "travel" well and that become decontextualized as they move across landscapes and locations, the situated meanings in the students' telenovela were blurred in its travel from children's lived knowledge to the classroom. When the students shared their telenovela with the class and collectively analyzed it, we (Carmen, Rocío, and Vivian as teacher-researchers) were immediately confused by the title. We initially thought it was about homeless people and insisted on clarification around their title. With some level of frustration with us, because we were obviously not getting it, they had to explain what the concept of "the street" meant, and that it was not what we thought. Instead they explained *barrio en la calle* means people who hang out on the streets as a lifestyle. "Porque no es un deambulante. Es que esta en la calle. Alguien que todo el tiempo esta en la calle y después cuando va a acostarse va a la casa." [Because he is not a homeless person. It's that he is on the streets. Someone who spends all the time on the streets and when he goes to sleep goes to his home.]

Still, as teachers, we left the discussion with a certain level of confusion. Furthermore, in addition to playing with the title, the students were also constructing a particular embodied performance situated in global imaginaries and this was also evident in their choice of characters T.I. and The Game. At first we did not pay much attention to the characters, but later on, when we realized that we were missing key knowledge to make sense of their text, Carmen decided to look up the characters' names on the Internet. She found that both T.I. and The Game are hip-hop artists from the U.S. and that the idea of experiencing life on the streets is at the core of their artistic and intellectual work. The Game and T.I. are described as artists whose work speaks of their experiences living in urban centers. More specifically, T.I. is a music artist, producer, and author of the book *Power and Beauty:*

A Love Story of Life in the Streets, who reminds his audience that "he is still street" (Harris, 2011). In the creation of these characters, the students make global references that also provide context for locating the narrative in their story in San Juan. Additionally, the relocalization of street is emphasized in their writing: they compose a text using a graffiti style and a particular graffiti style that has become popular in the streets of Puerto Rico. Through their writing style, they constructed a localized global connection that has become part of the local resources in the island "streets" and part of their repertoire of semiotic resources available to the children.

The students' telenovela storyline and multimodal composition, from a cultural production perspective, shows how in the students' playfulness with the text, they portray characters that are aligned to the larger globalized urban hip-hop imaginary relocalized in Puerto Rico. Nevertheless, what becomes interesting—and an important lesson in dominant classroom ways of doing literacy and its discourses—is the fact that the teacher-researchers did not have the knowledge to make sense of the children's work and this lack of knowledge on our part was obvious to the children. Interestingly in our analysis of their second draft, the children wrote a more elaborated plot but they lost the characters "T.I." and "The Game," replacing them with "la joven" [the young woman], "el joven" [the young man] and "el esposo" [the husband] and "la esposa" [the wife]. These two characters are generic and lack the depth of the previous ones. We remain curious about their decision and wonder how much our questioning of their text imposed our adult views and values and influenced their change of names.

CONVERGENCES AMONG CONSUMPTION CULTURES AND OTHER WAYS OF PLAYING WITH BEAUTY IMAGINARIES

After the inquiry unit on telenovelas was finalized, we decided to begin an inquiry unit on global dominant beauty discourses and its relation to local consumption cultures and practices. Through some productive and some not so productive moments that are beyond the scope of this book, we attempted to bring to the surface the multiple ways in which women were portrayed in global popular media and how that relates to our local consumer practices. Situated in Carrington's (2003) ideas around a glocalized model of literacy, the unit included:

- An analysis of alternative beauty representations in popular media
- A dramatic process experience of designing a commercial product
- A media campaign considering multiple critical perspectives and stances in how and why a product is advertised for consumption
- An analysis of print/visual Mother's Day advertisements of discounted products from global companies in the local newspapers in Puerto Rico

The curricular engagements around the analysis of multinational companies print/visual sale advertisements in local newspaper proved to be one of the most interesting aspects of the project. In Chapter 3, Carmen shared an ethnographic analysis of the overarching presence of multinational corporations in Puerto Rico, particularly around the cities close to the school. Through this ethnographic documentation, it was possible to see the material consequences of how global markets dominate the local economy and their strong influence on how local discourses around politics "of progress" are played out in Puerto Rico. The local newspaper plays a significant role on these global–local processes, particularly in the ways print literacy constructs and gets constructed around the proliferation of multinational markets and the creation of competitive markets through multimodal advertisements of products on sale. Puerto Ricans, in a society that traditionally has had a very high newspaper-reading cultural practice, get bombarded daily by hundreds of discounted product advertisements. We collected newspaper advertisements during Mother's Day weekend and brought those to the classroom. We worked with the children analyzing these advertisements (for stores such as Kmart, JCPenney, and Walmart) and explored the question: How are dominant representations of beauty use by corporate markets to sell products, including dominant views of Latinas? The following transcripts show a set of interactions between the teachers and students that depicts our beginning conversations and questionings:

- How are we implicated in the cycle of consumer culture and how do we engage in a critical conversation of who is present and absent?
- Who gets privileged and what are the intentions of this text in relation to my role as a reader/consumer?

Notice that the word *shopper* is used throughout the interactions to make reference to print media advertisements. This is the common term people in Puerto Rico used for this kind of print advertisement—a hybridization of language that hints at the linguistic and cultural glocalization that is part of the island's colonial history by inserting an English word into our everyday Spanish talk.

Transcript	Translation
Rocío: ¿Cómo son esos shoppers? ¿Que ustedes recuerdan de esos shoppers? ¿Cómo son esos shoppers de las tiendas?	Rocío: How are these shoppers? What do you remember about these shoppers? How are these store shoppers?
Carlos: Que cuando yo voy que encontramos algo y no se el precio, buscamos en el shopper y buscamos en la revista y dice el precio.	Carlos: That when I go to the store and I find something and I don't know the price we look in the shopper and we look in the booklet and it says the price.

(continued)

Transcript	Translation
Carmen: O sea que puedes buscar los precios.	Carmen: In other words, you can find the prices.
Carlos: De lo que esta en venta. De lo que tienen barato.	Carlos: Of what is on sale. Of what they have cheap.
Rocío: Y además de los artículos y lo que cuestan esos artículos ¿Que otras cosas hay en los shoppers?	Rocío: And in addition to the articles and how much these article cost, what other things are there in the shoppers?
Silencio	Silence
Ramón: ¿Cómo cual shopper?	Ramón: Like which shopper?
Maestra: ¿Cómo cual? Como el de Sears o el de JCPenney's.	Teacher: Like which one? Like the Sears or JCPenney's.

In this initial interaction, Carmen's co-researcher Rocío begins by opening the conversation to describe what *shoppers* are and what they look like. The children share their response and demonstrate a sense of agency as consumers; that is, they indicate they do not passively examine *shoppers* but they use them in "the store and I find something and I don't know the price we look in the shopper and we look in the booklet and it says the price." They know that these advertisements' texts serve as guides to search for products and prices and to compare "Lo que esta en venta. De lo que tiene barato." [Of what is on sale. Of what they have cheap]. From an agentic consumer's practice perspective, the students know how to purposively and strategically use these visual and print texts as part of the integrated practices of consuming products in a knowledgeable way. This was an important perspective for us to understand the complex set of actions and interactions that frame the multiple layers of reading these texts. Furthermore, we were still interested in the analysis of how these multinational commercial texts are constructed in relation to beauty, consumption, and power. Following is a small group interaction with the teacher, analyzing the advertisements.

Transcript	Translation
[*estudiantes ojean los "shoppers"*]	[*students browse* shoppers]
Carlos: Mira, mira esta es idéntica a la mamá de Juan.	Carlos: Look, look, this one is identical to Juan's mother.
Ramón: Aja.	Ramon: Aha.
Juan: Esa es Mónica la de *Muchachitas Como Tu*, la novela.	Juan: That is Monica from *Muchachitas Como Tu*, the telenovela.
Carlos: No, esta es como tu mamá.	Carlos: No, that is like your mom.

In this interaction, the boys are informally sharing what they see in the *shoppers* before the teacher initiates her formal teaching. The boys first make a connection between the physical appearance of one of the other boy's mothers and the model on the cover of the shopper. This interaction makes visible the global marketing strategy of using female and male models that "look like" Puerto Ricans to advertise their products. The relocalization dynamics in the print/visual text functions as a glocalized embodied representation to sell global market products using local resources such as Latina models that "look" like their mothers. Interestingly, they quickly moved to comparing the model with a character in the popular telenovela *Muchachitas Como Tu* [Teenage Girls Like You]. In this way, they moved smoothly from a local family connection to another global media connection. In some ways, this becomes a recursive process where we move in and out of the telenovela's world in relation to local consumption practices and dominant beauty discourses, particularly the idea that characters and models look "like you" as in the telenovela's title. The students' informal conversation hints at the many connections the students make between consumers' texts, media, and their everyday lives. This dialogue opens a new path for complicating literacy curricula as cultural production by using an inquiry lens where the globalized landscapes students bring to the classroom initiate other critical conversations and open up other possibilities for whose, how, and which converging worlds intersect in dynamic ways particularly in local communities.

SLIPPAGES AMONG TEACHERS' NOSTALGIC CHILDHOOD IMAGINARIES AND CHILDREN'S CONTEMPORARY MEDIA IMAGINARIES

In this section, Karen examines teachers' knowledge and decision-making in the context of her work with early childhood teachers in developing play-based literacy and filmmaking curricula, looking specifically at two early childhood teachers' selection of popular media toys for a filmmaking center in their preschool classroom. During the yearlong curriculum development project, teachers designed activities to help children access their media knowledge and collaboratively produce their own films. In the process, teachers also shared their concerns about developmentally appropriateness of media, pressures for academic achievement, and perceptions of parental beliefs about popular media. This section deals with a teaching team's decision to provide *Toy Story 3* figurines in the moviemaking center to encourage children to play and video-record stories using popular media.

The literacy potential of popular media toys for children's cultural production depends upon players' ability to draw upon their shared knowledge of popular media texts; however, popular media are often viewed as problematic in early childhood education as too sexual, violent, vulgar, or commercial for young children. In Chapter 3, we explored how transmedia flows connect each product with other commercial products within the scope of the brand and "with it their ideological messages and inducements to consumption, throughout our virtual and spatial environment, where our individual traversals will encounter it again and again" (Lemke, 2009, p. 292). After discussing the benefits and drawbacks of several brands, the teaching team decided to provide *Toy Story 3* miniature dolls in a moviemaking center. The teachers hoped that by providing the toys, they could avoid disadvantaging children who did not have media toys to bring from home. Furthermore, they deliberately chose the *Toy Story 3* franchise as the brand that they believed most parents might know and be more likely to accept. We can see how selecting a media franchise that featured old-fashioned, conservative toys helped teachers cope with a pervasive accountability discourse that monitors teachers' actions and decisions.

However, the decision to bring in *Toy Story 3* dolls and toys received a lukewarm reception from most children who had little knowledge of, connection to, or passion for the *Toy Story 3* film characters or narrative. Although the children were immediately interested in handling the toys, they quickly lost interest and did not engage in play around the media characters or film narratives. This was not surprising as the teachers' own informal inventory of children's transmedia (e.g., clothing, backpacks, school supplies) had identified Disney Princesses, Transformers, and Star Wars as dominant media interests, but the teachers perceived these transmedia as too overtly gendered or violent and contradictory to their shared developmentally appropriate discourse. The teachers felt that because they were providing the toys, they would be open to critique from parents or administers who might see such toys as inappropriate for school. How can we understand the teachers' selection of the *Toy Story 3* brand in view of the children's unfamiliarity with the Toy Story franchise, the primacy of our study group's overarching aim to build upon children's media expertise, and the preschool's mission to provide emergent curriculum that follows children's demonstrated interests?

Using the frame of children's cultural production in the context of global transmedia flows, it is possible to understand the teachers' choice of *Toy Story 3* as an adult consumerist reading of a brand. The Toy Story brand is a marker of wide acceptance, a flagship franchise produced by media giant Disney Pixar, recognized by the 2011 Academy Awards. The classic toys in the film activate adult nostalgia for childhood toys from the 1950s to 1980s (e.g., Mr. Potato Head, Slinky, Barbie, Ken, pink piggy bank, Howdy Doody–style cowboy and cowgirl stuffed dolls, super-powered astronaut action figure, plastic dinosaur, green soldier figurines). However, the brand and its "classic" toys also carry histories that challenge the teachers' assumptions about the franchise as "safe" and nongendered. Pixar has a masculinist tradition of male leads in buddy movies (e.g., *Shrek, Monsters, Inc.*), and this continues in the Toy Story franchise. Although a more active heroic cowgirl is added in the sequels, she is clearly a sidekick, while Woody and Buzz are the heroic leads, apparent in product packaging that features Woody and Buzz standing side by side. The (male) buddy message is amplified by color schemes that repeat the message that boys are target consumers: Woody and Buzz (only) appear on most products and Toy Story sky-blue products are often positioned as the alternative choice to Disney Princess pink products on store shelves and ads.

The emphasis on adult nostalgia in the franchise helps explain the disconnect between teachers' and children's media knowledge. The teachers' toy selection was constrained and bounded by an adult nexus of practice for appropriate teaching that ignored children's immersive media experiences, demonstrating how easily we can miss opportunities to help children connect their media knowledge to their potential literacy resources.

However, when teachers are careful kid-watchers, such misses can become ruptures that allow more opportunities to emerge—if we recognize the ways that we as educators are complicit in upholding nexus. In this case, the children's lackluster response to the toys led to critical discussion among the teachers about who the curriculum was really designed for. We discussed how teachers' assumptions about the appropriateness of children's toys in terms of gender or violence pivot on our own tacit beliefs about gender, class, and taste. The teachers then decided to bring in a more child-favored franchise and to provide ten Disney Princesses dolls and two digital cameras in the classroom play center. The teachers also mediated as co-players, suggesting alternate settings (e.g., swamps, garages) in hopes of encouraging children to imagine new and (less overtly gendered) narratives. Children were also encouraged to film their own stories, to build play sets with craft supplies, to add "found" materials from the classroom, and to make their own props and clothing for the dolls to prompt improvisation. The result was lots of play and small inroads toward rupturing the princess nexus. The preschoolers made many short exploratory films and played a few stories featuring princess dolls with switched clothing and names, including one with Snow White fighting a swamp monster spontaneously named "Delicate" by one of the children (Wohlwend, in press).

Providing princess dolls with the hope of reconstructing damsel-in-distress narratives is a meager beginning to critical inquiry and we could have taken our teacher-researcher discussions further to understand our complicity as educators. For example, we were much more comfortable trying to disrupt children's preferences for pink glittery plastic or princess dolls—through curricular activities that almost always fell flat—than in disrupting our adult-centric decisions and authority that provided natural wood materials, classic toys, and seemingly gender-free dolls.

CONCLUSION

In this chapter, we have explored how the emergence of cultural imaginaries is not limited or exclusive to popular culture experiences that children bring to the classroom. Although such resources clearly generate new ways of participating in literacy practices, they operate in complementary or contradictory ways with other global networks, such as educational systems and digital cultures, among others. Here, we explored some of these other cultural production dynamics in classrooms in Puerto Rico and Iowa, examining these through the lens of the cultural imaginary. Our intention in writing this chapter collaboratively and by looking across classroom experiences working with children and teachers is to provide a view of multiple sites of engagement where teachers encourage children to play and remake these imaginaries.

Part III

Convergences in Collective Cultural Imaginaries

In Part I and Part II, we presented theories of global–local dynamics of cultural production, particularly in relation to classroom practices that make visible the subtleties of how global networks and discourses interact in local contexts. In Part III, we return to the model presented in Part I (see Figure 2.1) to articulate and discuss the affordances and limitations of working on a literacy curriculum centered on play, dramatic experiences, and cultural production. A curriculum that foregrounds cultural production makes visible, explores, and generates knowledge in relation to the complex convergences children negotiate in their everyday lives, including their lived experiences in classrooms. In Chapter 7, we look across the classroom activities described in Chapters 4, 5, and 6 to delineate one possible way to envision classroom literacy work as aesthetic labor with cultural convergences that produce shared imaginaries. We argue that teaching to make spaces for imagination as social practice in contemporary times puts children's intercultural capital at the center of their literacy experiences. In Chapter 8, we examine children's cultural imaginaries, looking across these intersections to explore three interdependent components in children's critical cultural production within performance practices: imagination, convergence, and collaboration. In Chapter 9, we bring these ideas to teacher education, looking across our individual teaching in university classrooms and professional development to rethink teacher education.

7   Participation, Scripting, and Embodiment in Children's Collective Imaginaries

Our notion of converging collective imaginaries conceptualizes what is produced at the intersections of three kinds of cultural inquiry: ethnographies of globalization, nexus of practice, and performance (see Figure 2.1). As depicted in the model, we situate these three bodies of knowledge as overlapping to create an expansive view of classroom literacies in relation to (1) children's multiple sites of engagement (imagined communities); (2) the connected and expected cultural practices negotiated across sites (nexus of practice); and (3) the identity enactments, improvisations, and ruptures (performances) that emerge as converging imaginaries in children's multiliteracies work. In this chapter, we examine each of these intersections to understand what can be seen through its particular lens on children's cultural production.

PLACES, PRACTICES, AND PARTICIPATION

The multiple sites of cultural engagement children navigated in our studies (depicted in maps in Figures 3.1 and 3.3) demonstrate how complex and multilayered are the places, practices and forms of participation that are simultaneously available throughout different moments in the classrooms (Figure 7.1).

Working at the convergence of global cultural imaginaries, local cultural imaginaries, classroom cultural imaginaries, and media imaginaries, it is possible to understand engagement in cultural production in quite dynamic ways.

The classroom context as a *place* with routine *practices*, and the forms of *participation* that these practices invite or generate, becomes a location where the sedimented histories of schooling, popular culture, local community practices, and teachers' and students' identities intersect and interact. In Puerto Rico, the inquiry work on telenovelas in a third grade classroom is produced in relation to school practices and accountability discourses that mandate a national curricular basal reader and its accompanying practices that were mostly aligned with and driven by federal policies in the No Child Left Behind era. In Iowa, the play-based literacy around Disney

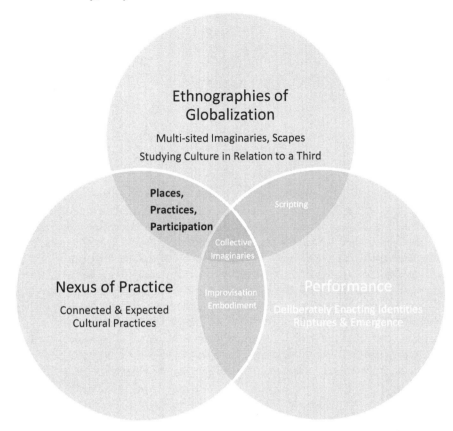

Figure 7.1 Intersection of ethnographies of globalization and nexus of practice: Places, practices, and participation.

Princess media was legitimated by discourses of individual choice and self-expression in a writing workshop approach to language arts but as a supplement to a local school district–adopted basal reading series. These school literacy programs function in relation to a third: a federal or local government that, while not there in the physical classroom, is materially present through materials, tools, practices, approaches, and discourses. These components interact with the teachers' discourses, tools, and practices around their individual commitments to develop critical literature-based curricula to supplement the mandated basal.

Although with limited resources, children in the Puerto Rico classroom had an opportunity to explore literature beyond the basal and to engage in meaningful discussions around authentic texts that created a different kind of literary community. Furthermore, this was in relation to the specific work we did reframing the critical literacy curriculum to foreground out-of-school literacies in relation to classroom work (what Carmen later defines as critical scripting). This became an opening to explore telenovelas as a site for engagement, interpretation, and meaning making of a media text that came with its own discourses, practices, and forms of participation. The trajectory and histories of telenovelas as common family practice of entertainment outside the classroom in the local community and through access to multiple texts (television, magazines, in doctor's offices or stores, online texts) brought in additional discourses and places. For example, dominant discourses of femininities, masculinities, and consumption were part of the repertoire of response and production practices that were generated in the classroom, which also permeated the ways we (teacher and researchers) devised and conceptualized curricular experiences. The boundaries of how these sites of cultural production intersected, were rejected, or were in opposition with one another also triggered other forms of knowledge, participation, histories, and identity texts beyond what teachers expected, such as those related to domestic violence and local social conditions.

In the physical place of the Iowa kindergarten, daily play periods produced a site of engagement that mingled a similar mix of gender, popular media, and school practices and discourses: hegemonic masculinities with nexus of practice based on physical skill and sports competitions among boys, emphasized femininities with nexus of practice that stressed princess play and dominant beauty ideals among girls. These discourses aligned with community discourses such as sports talk and competitive models among football fans that circulated dominant masculinities and media discourses that circulated a kind of hyperfeminine girlhood and Whiteness beauty ideals in Disney Princess media. Classrooms are sites of contestation, in part because of overlapping and conflicting practices and discourses that produce dilemmas for teachers who want to abide by institutional rules and work in ways that are consistent with their professional ethos (Wohlwend, 2009b). In the Iowa kindergarten, the school culture nexus of practice circulated contradictory educational models. Accountability discourse privileged print-centric practices that were measured and driven by standardized testing, imposed through federal mandates, which conflicted with other institutional discourses. Child-centered early childhood educational discourses, such as developmentally appropriate practice and a writing workshop approach to language arts, promoted active inquiry, learner-driven curriculum and cooperative interactions. Together these discourses supported classroom practices that set aside the basal and rigid curriculum requirements and made room for play as a space for children to engage in individual authorship, playful cooperation, and personal expression. A peer culture thrived in this play-rich atmosphere nourished by child-centered practices that allowed children the autonomy to sit where they chose, to form peer groups around their shared media interests, and, important to the purpose of productive critique, to engage and re-engage identity texts across these discourses on a daily basis. However, it's important to recognize that the same child-centered discourses that enabled play also provided the space for children to emphatically reinscribe gendered boundaries and exclusionary peer social hierarchies.

Across settings and classroom contexts, patterns of participation became ingrained in the playgroups and dramatic performance troupes that children formed and repeatedly worked in over time. Stable groups allowed players to develop and come to recognize their shared artifacts as specific meaning holders that symbolized or pointed to particular practices or identities and to build up shared nexus of practice for the recontextualized "as if" play worlds they imagined.

Conflicts and negotiations were key to these collaborations: in unsettling the regular ways of being and doing, in securing agreement among all players, and in producing new directions for storytelling—overall in clarifying and thus making visible and malleable the tacitly valued practices in the many nexus of practice that overlap in a performance nested in a peer group in a classroom site in a community and so on.

SCRIPTING IDENTITY TEXTS: THE ROLE OF THE IMAGINATION AS A SOCIAL PRACTICE

In the process of producing work at the intersection of global–local networks of places, a focus on practices, participation, and discourses helps us understand the role of the imagination as a social practice, as Appadurai defines it. *Scripting*, or imagination as a social practice, allows us to reimagine a literacy curriculum where interpretation, production, and recontextualization all work as the engine to produce curricular encounters where children are repositioned in relation to agency and their work as cultural producers and interpreters (Figure 7.2). Their engagement in improvisational work as "aesthetic labor" was produced at the juxtaposition of texts, identities, and desires while recontextualizing through a multiplicity of cultural resources. These dynamics are produced in the classroom in interaction with school literacy routines and approaches such as critical literacy approaches that reposition readers as social actors or a writer's workshop in a play-based classroom where children produce work as authors, actors, and directors.

As we look across our studies, we can see the workings of a curriculum that makes visible how echoes of global power circulate in relation to media in local communities and classrooms. What is important in scripting global media is our (students', teachers', and researchers') collective ability to work with possibilities and contradictions and to use those as ways to reflect and move the inquiry process forward. Within this complexity, as social media theorists argue (Strelitz, 2003), it is possible to see the subtle mediations interplaying in people's relationships with media that need to be located in the wide range of sociopolitical landscapes that people negotiate.

In the telenovelas work, the children were able to make visible and reflect in the space between literary texts and telenovelas' sociopolitical

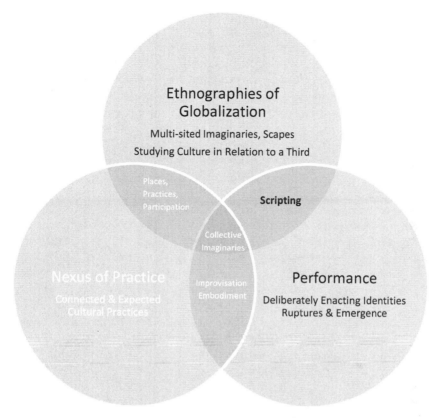

Figure 7.2 Intersection of ethnographies of globalization and performance: Scripting.

landscape. While the everyday lived practice of watching a telenovela could be perceived as a superficial or mundane activity, in the classroom it was repositioned as a collective site for action and cultural production to understand the critical relationship between media and notions of belonging inside or outside dominant discourses of beauty. The curricular inquiry on telenovelas worked as a way to map the complex social ecology of telenovelas' discourses as texts with levels of interconnectivity and how those serve as lenses to understand local–global social conditions. As the students read between *Paper Bag Princess* and telenovelas, in their writing and production of telenovelas and in their critical analysis of their authored telenovelas, scripting was at the core of how social practices got improvised, reinvented, and produced in new contexts.

In the kindergarten classroom, children both reproduced and revised scripts in popular media—literally as they rewrote princess film scripts to fit their diverse lived experiences and interests—but also as they rescripted the implicit scripts—the expectations, actions, and relationships created through their new identity texts. During "Scary Godmother" play, boys could open up who plays what so that they could imagine themselves as Cinderella or Fairy Godmother. Just as important, the boys could recruit players to join them in these new scripts and convince other children to accept their princess performances as valid. Similarly, Jenna could imagine otherwise, by creating fairy-tale families with same-sex parents that more closely resembled her own lived experience. Scripting during cooperative play opened up possibilities and allowed children to challenge the tacitly accepted identity texts for playing princesses and princess fans while enacting boys or girls in the peer and school cultures. In this classroom, the opportunity to play a script with others opened negotiations of identity but also affirmed children's cultural experiences as important sources of literary material, bridging home and school resources. The key to critical cultural production was the opportunity to play identity texts with and against other children's performances of related identity texts. As they experienced tensions among commercially given scripts and their desires and knowledges, players improvised beyond conflicts and invented new identities, such as Cinderella's brothers. Of course, children could also wield their intercultural capital in impromptu competitions to test the weight of an Aladdin song against the heft of reported CD wealth, to imagine "I got a hundred of 'em," and to renegotiate what is possible in order to belong, that is, to rescript the rules for participating while negotiating together.

IMPROVISATION AND EMBODIMENT: COMPOSING HISTORICAL AND IMAGINED BODIES

A nexus of practice lives in historical bodies, ingrained in the "muscle memory" of past practices that are so familiar they are almost automatic. This embodied "ordinariness" gives nexus its power, as these well-known practices are expected and handed down as norms. These are unmarked, and therefore unremarkable, ways of behaving or acting with bodies. When nexus of practice intersect with deliberate performances of identity—as happens in play and dramatization—these unmarked ways of acting are exaggerated, manipulated, and made available for remaking according to the players' purposes and interests (Figure 7.3). *Improvisation* allows children to appropriate, mix, stretch, and even exploit the "normal" identity texts in a given nexus of practice into performances that fit their immediate purposes: provide more entertaining storylines, wield cultural capital, or gain access to a playgroup or favorite toy, and so on.

Performance produces an interactive script within a collectively imagined cultural context in which players contribute their bodies and agree to allow others to co-determine their own actions as they create and maintain a cohesive play narrative. Pretend play with popular media adds another dimension as emotional connections are evoked when children play the

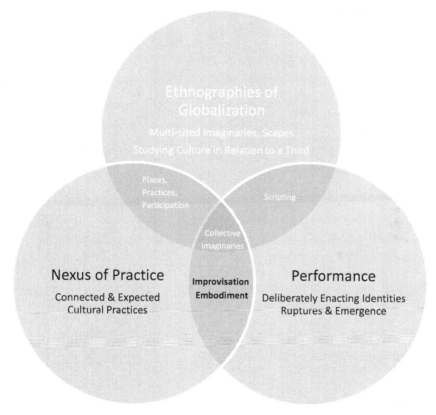

Ethnographies of
Globalization

Multi-sited Imaginaries, Scapes
Studying Culture in Relation to a Third

Places,
Practices,
Participation

Scripting

Collective
Imaginaries

Nexus of Practice

Improvisation
Embodiment

Performance

Connected & Expected
Cultural Practices

Deliberately Enacting Identities
Ruptures & Emergence

Figure 7.3 Intersection of nexus of practice and performance: Improvisation and embodiment.

characters and places they love in the nexus they know, practice, and recognize in each other.

In the kindergarten, children engaged in spontaneous embodied forms of collaborative composing through play. They took up and lived in embodied identity texts as they performed Disney narratives, in ways that made gendered nexus of practice more available for reinterpretation and remaking. It is this malleability that offers rich potential for critical engagement as children could fluidly reshape a princess character's typical actions or expected traits or reassign who could be an "appropriate" player by convincing other players to agree to pretend. It is important to note that this critical work took place in a space of relative safety and pleasure, where acting otherwise was expected and could be laughed off as silly. However, that is not to say that there was no pain or that play negotiations were not hard-fought. There were sometimes tears over who could or could not join a playgroup, enact a beloved character, or play the role of mother with the power to direct others. Embodiment captures the materiality as well as emotional capacity that come with acting with bodies: gestures, postures, physical movements, and emotional responses.

In closing this chapter, we would like to say that media (like other globalized phenomena and networks) is one way in which imagined worlds are created through people's participation in shared cultural practices that cannot be located in one place but that have an effect on the production of localities (geographical and imagined). The Latino television genre of telenovelas has been described as a cultural media narrative where people's desires and aspirations become part of a common interpretative space across members of multiple communities in Latin America, the U.S., or Africa (Orozco-Gomez, 2006). This becomes apparent in children's practices watching, playing with, and producing multinational Spanish telenovela shows. Similarly, young children often used Disney Princess play to imagine fairy-tale dramas through collaborative pretense and design. These media scenarios allowed children to enact identities and relationships that would not otherwise be available to students in classrooms. More important, participation and membership in these imagined worlds do not produce shared worlds of passive consumption. The new cultural economy created through media (media reception studies have a long history of research on this subject) includes participation in these imagined worlds where shared meanings are mediated and are not neutral. From these perspectives, a nexus of participation in "collective imaginaries" includes the ways people can connect with others (physically, digitally, through shared media experiences) to engage, participate, make sense, and/or move across one or multiple imagined worlds and its cultural practices.

8 Globalization, Imagination, and the Possibilities of Agency

In this chapter, we identify three interdependent components in children's critical cultural production within performance practices: imagination, convergence, and collaboration. We work across these three aspects to lay out and make an argument for an approach to classroom literacy work as cultural production for two purposes: (1) as a means to resituate engagement and learning in ways that align with children's encounters with literacy in their everyday lives and (2) as a way to reposition classrooms as part of these practices. This positions classrooms as key places to produce new localities for learning instead of classrooms as isolated or separate entities where knowledge is predetermined. In this interpretation, we look to sociologists of globalization and Hannerz's (1996) description of "habitats of meaning" to describe the ways we engage with multiple texts and practices in playful ways that go beyond geographical locations. We argue that classrooms should be approached as another habitat functioning within and against the multiple flows, translocalities, and identity performances children engage within and outside classrooms.

IMAGINATION AS A MEDIATOR OF GLOBALIZATION

The challenge in creating pedagogies that respond to contemporary global flows is the difficulty of working with the speed, fluidity, and complexity in which networks overlap, knowledge is produced, and dominant discourses spread out. But the same forces that produce this challenge—speed, fluidity, and complexity—are also the affordances of improvisation that make playful and dramatic performance pedagogies so powerful. These resonances, or "echoes," as described in globalization studies (García-Canclini, 1995; Murphy & Kraidy, 2003), with global flows make imagination an apt tool for critically engaging globalization dynamics. Its mediating potential is clear when we contrast improvisation with other educational strategies to cope with globalization. For example, schools attempt to manage digital flows by continually updating school equipment to stay ahead of spiraling technology or by trying to safeguard children from expansive social networks by building firewalls and filters and by keeping popular media out of classrooms.

As educators, we must first accept that we cannot control globalization, but that we can facilitate pedagogies to imagine and produce alter-global perspectives. The discourse of control, one of the pillars of schooling, is often the default response of educational institutions and policy makers, evident in classroom discipline programs and student behavior policies: The goal becomes keeping students under control and restricting resources so that activities cannot move beyond school surveillance. However, control is not learning. We argue that a learning focus must look beyond control and that improvisation provides a way of moving past futile attempts to keep up with or to contain global flows and to instead make use of the affordances, complexities, problems, and contradictions of globalization. In this sense what we learned and what we laid out at the beginning of the book from the sociology of globalization is critical in our understanding of how to think of practices that allow for the creative, the political, and the agentic to coexist (or what Appadurai defines as scripting) in ways that account for the histories, spaces, and temporalities that emerge in border crossings and hybrid locations. We see improvisation as an incubator for the "as if," a space-making practice that produces imaginaries, and an act of cultural production that welcomes ruptures and the emergence of alternatives as knowledge is produced within and between multiple sites of engagement. In performance practices in the classroom, such as play and dramatic experiences, a context is created for complex border crossings to happen in action. Both the telenovelas and Disney chapters are examples of these dynamics. These actions are not stable and usually permeate to other classroom events that get framed and reframed by the multiple localities and discourses constructed within play and dramatic experiences. This is the case in the telenovelas chapter where teacher-researchers' curricular decisions became hybridized across discourses and locations situated in the children's production of telenovelas, their everyday social conditions, the gender constructs of media, and the literacy inquiry curricula.

In some ways, imagination is the antithesis of control. Improvisation is messy, just as globalization is messy. If as Santos suggests, globalization functions within complex power dynamics where globalizing local practices become homogenous and localizing homogenous global practices become new locals—in other words, a nexus of practice—then our pedagogical approaches to children's engagement with texts in their everyday lives must provide spaces for the negotiation, renegotiation, and emergence that children mediate in their encounters with globalization. The performativity (Dolan, 1993)—the ways we interact and enact identities and discourses in relation to the cultural conventions of the multiple geographies we move through—that occurs in improvisation repositions children as cultural workers within the classroom, a perspective that is quite different from a view of literacy practices as skills consumption and reproduction where children are passive. Similar to critical researchers who reject characterizations of media consumption as a passive activity, we want to disrupt the view of literacy as passive consumption of text and move into a dynamic, collective, and improvisational space where new ideas are produced and strategized within and in between play and dramatic performances.

Imagining alternatives is a productive response to globalization that reinvents a glocalized nexus of practice. The nexus of practice is the cultural given that supplies the well-known roles and authorized scripts that improvisation pushes against, twists, or remakes in collaboration with others. We must find ways of bringing naturalized nexus out into the open and making glocalized practices visible and questionable, available for collective critique and remaking in ways that rupture expectations and produce new nexus. In order to reimagine the known into something new, we need spaces where players can play and improvise together and where their collaborative critical action is supported. Classrooms can be these kinds of transformational sites, but that is not to suggest that this work will be easy, safe, or unproblematic. When we open play and dramatic experience spaces and encourage players to improvise on dominant realities, children raise tough questions that are political or that feel dangerous, perhaps too dangerous for teachers to deeply engage with students in classrooms. Imagining otherwise as a social practice feels uneasy and risky, and we wonder if we should back away. This is the space of improvisation, prompted by an uncomfortable convergence and ruptured nexus of practice. It is the heart of play and dramatic experiences—improvisation that takes risks and spins out in unpredictable ways—rather than the romanticized vision of children cooperating and giggling in harmonious pretense.

We recognize play and dramatic experiences as powerful means of collective cultural production. We conceptualize play and drama as a collaborative literacies that produce shared meanings in embodied texts. We also recognize the agentic potential of these literacies as tactics for reimagining cultural contexts (Wohlwend, 2011). When children play together, they imagine familiar cultural spaces into the classroom and make a broader range of diverse literacy practices available for enactment. This approach moves well beyond notions of agency as honoring children's topical interests by allowing popular media into school as a way to motivate them to write more and to enrich the school writing curricula. Furthermore, it troubles the idea of writing as an individualistic achievement, with each writer held accountable to nexus of practice governed by expectations shaped by rubrics of traits on standardized assessments. Such approaches subordinate play and drama in the service of writing.

By contrast, dramatic play and performance as literacies require ongoing cooperation among players who must work together to create and maintain a pretend situation (Corsaro, 2003; Heathcote, 1984, Sawyer, 2003). Collaborative literacies create productive tensions between the constraints of establishing and maintaining shared meanings and the affordances of pooling creative resources and moving meanings within and across spaces and imaginaries. Collaboration is forged in tensions among the need for shared understandings, the dynamic interpretations from multiple perspectives of players/readers, and the productive remaking of actively constructing a narrative together. Fluid recontextualizations, whether in young children's play, drama, text interpretations, writing, or design, bring the tacit expectations of nexus in the here-and-now into a negotiated and creative space where they bump against the nexus of expectations in global imaginaries. The ruptures and proliferations of converging practices produce openings where children can negotiate and improvise ways of belonging in these worlds. We want to be clear that literacies often work together to open spaces for collaborative cultural production: that is, neither reading, writing, designing, nor playing is privileged over the other, but combine in assemblages of literacies in moment-to–moment interactions. When children play and engage imagined worlds through dramatized assemblages of literacies, this rescripting produces a contested and transformative space, dense with opportunities for children to improvise and productively use power.

AGENCY WITHIN AND BETWEEN MICRO TACTICS AND CIRCULATING MACRO GLOBAL NETWORKS

The cultural imaginaries that are evoked and produced as productive responses to the scope and fluidity of places, or the ideas of places, provide more than an adaptation to the complexity of global flows converging in multiple sites, leading us to an appreciation of their value in proliferating resources and ruptures for the work of cultural production. The sites are multiply resourced with semiotic, material, and sociopolitical networks; yet this of course does not mean that subjects simply choose what to appropriate or how to participate. Social practices, naturalized yet purposeful ways of interacting, shape how social actors engage the stuff of everyday life. Understanding cultural imaginaries as glocalized and converging figured worlds, first described in ethnographies by Holland and colleagues (1998) but also described in the trajectory of work on anthropology of globalization (Marcus, 1995; Murphy & Kraidy, 2003; Appadurai, 1996), allows us to fit the construct of agency into dynamic and multiple spheres.

We find it useful to consider first a perspective on agency as micro tactics of everyday makings and remaking in human-scale ordinary engagements (de Certeau, 1984). This way of thinking about imagination as a mediator of global networks requires an expanded vision for ways of meaningfully engaging the world that encompasses literacy as embodied uses and small remakings with transmedia in everyday opportunities provided through converging collision, contestations, and so on. These convergences and contestations and the micro remakings that take place in scripting are also working and functioning in relation to macro global networks that have a material presence, that are relocalized in communities such as the ones in Iowa and Puerto Rico, and that circulate as "echoes of global power" in people's everyday lives.

Agency in this view is the ability to make use of the opportunities—clashes, collisions, slippages, and ruptures—that cultural convergences provide:

- By mustering multiple cultural semiotic resources to produce a collective imaginary.
- By recruiting co-players to renegotiate realities in terms of potentials.
- By recontextualizing the present moment to make it more accessible and malleable.
- By relocalizing and reinterpreting homogenous dominant discourses in relation to players' immediate social conditions (localizing globalization) to open the possibility of unpacking and mapping the complex ideological and power structures of globalization that have different consequences for different worlds, communities, and people.

Functioning within the micro tactics of agency that we described above, we also see circulating macro politics of globalization that have an effect across the communities and worlds that children lived in and engaged with. In this sense, the ethnographic work conducted outside the classroom served as a way to understand the material ways in which globalization functions within a community, whether in Puerto Rico or Iowa, through telenovelas or Disney. This is a perspective where we see much potential for pushing beyond what we present in this book. In the field of literacy, we still have much work to do to understand the possibilities of critical literacy not as a set of strategies but as strategizing practices, including within play and dramatic experiences, in relation to children's immediate lives, including the outside politics of globalization circulating in their local realities and its impact in the social conditions in which they live. We aim to continue pushing the boundaries of our political work in relation to globalization and hopefully other literacy scholars and educators will continue to do so, too.

CONVERGENCE AS A CATALYST FOR THE EMERGENCE OF NEW LOCALS

Envisioning convergence as a catalyst for the emergence of new locals is another significant aspect of framing the potential of improvisation within literacy play and dramatic experiences. The debate over what is global and local and how these interact are topics of much theorization within the field of anthropology and sociology (we explored some of these ideas in Part I). What emerged in our analysis gives us a better understanding of the process of theorization around globalization and the emergence of new locals. What becomes important to consider are the dynamics of:

1) What is produced in a situated moment of engagement with global networks?
2) What relocalizations emerge?
3) How do these moments of engagement become new localizations?

For us, convergence creates the possibility of critical response when overlapping multiple nexus of practice authorize multiple identity texts and scripts, producing dilemmas, squeezes, and ruptures and creating impossible situations and double binds that individuated actors feel compelled to resolve (Wohlwend, 2009b). In this way, convergence enables an unsettling. Where the dominant nexus and glocalized discourses in a site compete, norms and naturalized practices can be made less certain and open to multiple interpretations. This interdiscursivity creates ambiguity where openings emerge. When players meet these pressures within performance spaces, they can use improvisation as a tool to escape, resulting in the emergence of possibilities.

Further, performance itself creates convergence by generating multiple identity texts and scripts within imagined spaces layered on here-and-now classrooms, intentionally producing other realities and identities in tension with the given and the routine. This is more than just reclaiming the local space; it's purposeful cultural production and appropriation, seizing a potential, making it a locality, and playing it into a context that is visible, negotiable, and inhabitable. As we are able to provide a space for these networks and flows to land somewhere, the local becomes even more powerful as a possible space for more complex conversation and practice.

Thus, the resistance/rupture potential is in the convergence of multiple imaginaries: the cultural production of new localities and new identities and, more important, opportunities to play out and test out the ways these combinations work. In this way, the improvisational space becomes the new locality. In play and drama, and other literary forms, we seek out tensions to make storylines more interesting, to give actors and audience an exciting cultural space to explore, and to keep co-players engaged in the hard work of collectively maintaining an imagined space. So play and drama provides a creative space for an imaginary or new locality and a way to mediate the tensions in children's lives to make sense of real cultural issues. At the same time, these cultural tensions enliven play, keeping it interesting and compelling enough for messy collaborations. These productive interests—creative, cultural, and literary—engage all players and keep them engaged enough to continue negotiating to keep up the imaginary worlds.

Furthermore, diversity is an impetus for and a product of improvisation as possible roles and plots are animated and potential identities and spaces proliferate. In each opportunity to improvise, things become less homogeneous (moving away from dominant globals) and more diverse (moving toward situated locals). For example, some identity texts are produced by media designers for children, but there are also identity texts that children create and improvise from media characters and advertising images. Still other identity texts emerge from lived experiences in cultural worlds. These texts can be mergers or remakings of extant texts that attach a lived reality to a character identity, such as when a new identity text was created when children remade a mother struggling with a drunken father in a telenovela. Furthermore, in play, the new text is made meaningful in collaboration with others, renegotiated and agreed upon as others interact and bring their own character interpretations and lived experiences to another player's reading/ playing of an identity text. In this way, improvisation is always a collaboration and a production of diversity, conflicts, and possibilities.

9 Literacy, Play, and Globalization in Teacher Education
Critical Scriptings and Playshops

Frequently we are asked about the implications of our research in teacher education, both with teacher candidates and in-service teachers. This chapter is a reflective space where both authors explore how our work in literacy education with practitioners has been transformed by the ideas we presented in this book, particularly as it relates to new approaches to literacy teacher education and the ways we engage in teacher research by working with in-service teachers in their classrooms. It serves as our concluding chapter to share not so much a model but a lens and set of experiences to help us rethink literacy teacher education in relation to the negotiation of in- and out-of-school literacies, global and local practices and knowledges, and the possibilities for a generative literacy pedagogy in teacher education. Such pedagogies are grounded in experiencing our relationships to globalized networks and discourses and recognizing the ways we are implicated and actively participating in relocalizing, remaking, and reconstructing meanings around these relationships.

In this sense the idea of converging collective imaginaries in classroom cultural production that we introduced in Part I also informs our work with teachers. We perceive the bodies of knowledge in ethnographies of globalization, nexus of practice, and performance theory (see Figure 2.1) useful not only in framing critical research but also in creating an expansive view of literacy teacher education. In this process, we work with teachers and teacher candidates to recognize cultural production as the ways they: (1) navigate across multiple sites of engagement and imagined communities, (2) participate in connected and expected cultural practices negotiated across sites (nexus of practice), and (3) perform identities that emerge as converging imaginaries and new sites for scripting in their multiliteracies work. We work around these perspectives within two overlapping ideas that frame our individual work and that we have been developing over a number of years and research studies. For Carmen, this is the idea of shifting the notion of critical literacy strategies into *critical scriptings*, and, for Karen, this is the idea of moving from reading/writing workshops to literacy *playshops* in early childhood education. Both ideas have become critical components in our pedagogy as we teach and conceptualize curricular experiences at the teacher education level that are parallel to the practices we engage and investigate with children. The notions of *critical scriptings* and *playshops* overlap in many ways but also have distinctive characteristics. In constructing cultural imaginaries through performance with teachers, the different approaches of critical scriptings and playshops share unifying elements of inquiry that we frame here as guiding questions:

- What emerges through exploration of sites of engagement?
- How do imaginaries mediate multiple nexus?
- What does performance provide for cultural formations?
- How do imaginaries mediate literacy pedagogy?
- How do imaginaries construct new locals?

In Table 9.1, we share key elements of our two approaches to respond to these questions and provide an overview of each approach. Then, in the following section, we give examples from Carmen's critical scriptings in teacher education classes and Karen's teacher inquiry groups on creating classroom playshops, looking across our work with preservice and in-service teachers to highlight the convergences that connect to critical scriptings and playshops.

Table 9.1 Reframing Teacher Education: Critical Scriptings and Playshops

Critical Scriptings	*Playshops*
What emerges through exploration of sites of engagement?	
• Explorations make available children's cultural resources for remaking. • Remakes become openings for situated critical conversations and performances.	• Explorations encourage children to bring in and play cultural resources within child culture. • Replayings recombine texts and identities, creating slippages in children's media texts.
How do imaginaries mediate multiple nexus?	
• Expand and trouble participation in nexus. • Make discourses accessible for rupturing and remaking. • Share in participant's emerging imaginaries. • Enable embodied engagement as social actors.	• Expand participation by layering pretend and classroom nexus. • Make discourses accessible for exploring, slipping, and expanding. • Share in children's emerging imaginaries. • Enable multimodal engagement with artifacts and bodies.

(continued)

Table 9.1   (continued)

Critical Scriptings	Playshops
What does performance provide for cultural production?	
Dramatic experiences	Play
• Foreground collective creation and improvisation. • Evoke imagination as a social and critical practice. • Use bodies, cameras, and artifacts as tools.	• Allows children to work on a text by playing characters within a play text. • Negotiates and improvises coauthored meanings built moment to moment. • Uses bodies, toys, artifacts, and cameras as tools.
How do imaginaries mediate literacy pedagogy?	
Storying	Storying
• Blurs cultural production as text-making or text-making as cultural production. • Makes texts durable but always open for revision. • Acknowledges drafts and multiple versions of a story as valid. • Storying is what we make in the process and not just in the product. • Attends to dramatic structures: character, plot, dialogue, setting.	• Expands literacy to include embodied action (e.g., play, animation, filmmaking). • Makes durable always/already slippery pretense. • Acknowledges multiple replayings as valid drafting and revising process in a move away from workshop processes of drafting, polishing, publishing. • Sediments play meanings into artifacts (props, puppets, toys, videos).
Collaboration	Collaboration
• Hallmark of participatory literacies. • Collectively strategizing in literacy vs. individual literacy strategies.	• Hallmark of participatory literacies. • Generates collective agreed-upon meanings. • Enables response to action texts and other players in multiplayer pretense, live-action dramas, or films.
How do imaginaries construct new locals?	
• Acknowledge social experiences as scripts. • Play across places, temporalities, and cultural imaginaries. • Provide tactics for transformation through improvisation.	• Include digital technologies to connect new locals to global flows. • Produce and not just consume transmedia. • Recognize child-produced alternatives to media.

CRITICAL SCRIPTINGS IN TEACHER EDUCATION: FROM STRATEGIES TO STRATEGIZING

Over the past three years, Carmen has begun to shift and incorporate new pedagogical practices that reframe performance pedagogies and the emergence of formations across local and global discourses in her literacy methods courses. She calls this pedagogical experience *critical scriptings*, grounded in her work and theorization where pedagogical practices foreground the work of the imagination as a social practice. The goal of engaging in *critical scriptings* is to implicate, locate, and complicate ourselves within the complex politics and identity performances of local and global discourses in literacy pedagogies. Similar to the work presented in Chapter 4 on telenovelas, the goal here is to move away from notions of critical literacy engagement as a set of strategies to critical literacy engagement as scripting practices that are collectively produced and strategized in classrooms. The shift from the noun "strategies" into the action "scripting" provides a dynamic and anthropological lens for thinking of emerging cultural formations as an active process in which children and teachers (both in-service and teacher candidates) collectively engage in doing and experiencing reading, writing, performing, and exploring in their engagement in classroom literacy events.

In dramatic explorations in undergraduate language arts courses and graduate seminars, Carmen's objective has been to create a performative space in the classroom where she and her students explore the multiple perspectives and politics embedded in our relationships with global and local networks and discourses. In these performative spaces, we actively explore what naturalized nexus of practice become visible in our actions, how those nexus of practice become available for critique, and what possible remakings or new scripts for exploring other forms of participation emerge through dramatic encounters. She works against the idea that teacher education is about the process of learning how to educate "the other" to an approach to teacher education as identity work and cultural production that is about examining our own politics and ways of making meaning as active literate beings in society (Britzman, 1991; Medina & Costa, 2010). The following example of how these dynamics take place illustrates what she means by the idea of *critical scriptings* in practice.

One example of engagement in *critical scriptings* experiences is inspired by a reading of the wordless picture book *El Soldadito de Plomo (The Little Tin Soldier)*, by Jorg Muller (2005). In this text, Muller shares a contemporary version of Hans Christian Andersen's classic in which the little tin soldier travels across geographical locations; in Muller's innovation, the little tin soldier is accompanied by Barbie. Carmen's interpretation of the storyline based on the book images is as follows: The tin soldier is initially found under the floor of a house that has just been restored, in what seems like a Western middle-class neighborhood. The tin soldier is given to a child, apparently from a White European background, and becomes part of a toy collection, where the tin soldier "joins" Barbie. The child grows up, and together, Barbie and the tin soldier, eventually get thrown away and end up in a garbage bag on the streets of an urban center, where they both fall into an underground sewer. They travel down the sewer into a large river or ocean where they are eaten by a fish that eventually gets caught by a fisherman. The fisherman cleans the fish and both toys, the tin soldier and Barbie, are thrown away in a garbage Dumpster somewhere in an African country. A Black African woman picks them up from the Dumpster and gives the toys to a child who will clean them and redress them (in what seems like a traditional African textile). An adult helps the child build a tin car for the child to play with the tin soldier and Barbie. Eventually, a tourist in town meets the boy and buys the tin soldier, Barbie, and the tin play car. All three artifacts end up in an African toy collection in a Western city museum of international toys.

As we have explored in previous chapters, Muller's book, like the tele-novelas or Disney toys, can be perceived as having both potential and problems in its representation of characters and situations and its place in the classroom. Nevertheless, if the text is positioned as an "identity text" (Wohlwend, 2009a, 2012), embedded with histories of meanings, makings, uses, and discourses (including political), then the possibilities of opening up the text for interpretation and remakings in the classroom are multiple. The text then becomes a generative tool to engage in *critical scriptings* to play with and to construct other cultural imaginaries around ideas related to transnational moves, dominant globalization politics, and artifacts' histories and trajectories across worlds.

The following curricular exploration makes visible the relationship between places, temporalities, practices, and participation by focusing on making everyday artifacts "strange" to understand how "objects signal essential dimensions of lived realities" (Rowsell, 2011, p. 334). Instead of working with the text and the literal storyline (i.e., how Barbie and the tin soldier travel and carry meanings across a European or African country), Carmen decided to propose a new space for exploration where the text works as a background or pre-text (O'Neill, 1995) to trigger a performative experience that centers in the students' reflections and renegotiations of artifacts in their lives and the politics embedded in those relationships. In small groups, the students (in this section, Carmen uses the word *students* to refer to preservice and in-service teachers in their roles as students enrolled in college courses or workshops) identify an everyday artifact to work with. The artifact can either be there in the classroom or they can draw a picture of the artifact. The only requirement is that it cannot be some kind of "sacred" or "special" artifact (although the boundaries of sacred vs. mundane can be very blurred). The more mundane, the better. Students in their small groups are then invited to write on small strips of paper: three words that describe the artifact personally, three words that describe the artifact culturally, and three words that describe the artifact politically. Working on this dramatic exploration across places like Vancouver in British Columbia, Toronto in Ontario, El Paso in Texas, or Bloomington in Indiana, it is interesting to see the overlaps and uniqueness in the students' work. It is interesting because the work that emerges across places suggests a number of things, such as the students' complex participation in global economies, the uniqueness that transpire in the students' choosing an artifact that can be more locally situated or an artifact the hints at both local and global meanings. For example, common artifacts across places have been bottles of water (both plastic or reusable), Starbucks coffee cups, mobile phones, and laptop computers but also some unique artifacts like a teakettle a group of teachers explored in Vancouver or flip-flops explored during summer in Toronto.

In this first exploration—writing personal, cultural, and political words—the idea is for the students to take an ordinary artifact and set it up in a new space, to remove it from the ordinary, to make it "strange," and play with its multiple meanings. For example, selecting a teakettle in Vancouver was an interesting choice as the students described the artifact in very pragmatic ways and represented the role of tea drinking in their everyday lives while also presenting the historical and political ways that a teakettle hints at the colonial relationship between Canada and Britain and the world politics of fair trade around tea distribution and its consumption. The choice of a Starbucks coffee cup across classroom sites such as in Toronto or El Paso is also an interesting representation as the students create meanings around a multinational corporation that has impacted the ways we consume coffee in many places around the world (See also Scollon, 2001). Here it is important to see how the idea that artifacts hold histories and evoke memories (Rowsell, 2011) that relate to personal, cultural, and political performances that are usually normalized in our everyday lives (nexus of practice) becomes visible through these active explorations.

The following engagement is centered in an improvisation around the creation of a museum installation. Using what's available in the classroom (chairs, tables, book bags, computers, or any other artifact available, etc.), the students arrange and set up the artifact and words as if it were a setup for a museum installation. The idea of the museum installation actually comes from the picture book read—*The Little Tin Soldier*—and it is a fascinating cultural and temporal space to explore. The museum provides the possibility of working across time: Is the museum situated in a future display of an artifact that was used in the "past" but that in reality is an artifact we use in our present? The possibility of playing across time resituates artifacts, their meanings, and politics across cultural imaginaries where we can improvise and reflect from a distance on a range of possible emergent discourses around our actions in the present. Furthermore, museums function as cultural and political spaces and we bring dominant discourses of what constitutes an "ideal" installation.

This experience serves as an opportunity to think of social practices related to the artifacts, time, and places in imaginative ways. Within the museum experience, students in each group have to create a five-minute improvisation where a museum tour guide describes the artifact to a group of visitors (the other people in the small group). The improvisation doesn't have to be highly framed; otherwise it loses its improvisational qualities. Instead students in each group are encouraged to get a general sense of what the improvisation will be about and to determine a starting and closing sentence. (This is mostly done in order to keep track of time.) In these improvisations, the students begin scripting political meanings related to their everyday interactions with the artifact that in the majority of the cases become cynical performances of their everyday actions. For example, the idea of buying bottled water is usually problematized with certain tones of cynicism as the students improvise scenes of the museum tour guide explaining how people "in the past" felt that buying a bottle of water gave them status or made them "look cool." The museum visitors who are part of the improvising group usually act astonished by the fact that people actually did/do that. The rest of the class observing the improvisation usually laughs at the visibility of absurdity in our everyday lives as politics and cultural meanings are inscribed in the improvisation. Sometimes the students' improvisations within the museum "in the future" reflect on how things have changed "in the present" and how a particular practice like buying bottled water has disappeared. In this moment, the imaginative engagement serves to articulate a new script that envisions other ways of being and participating, different from what's normalized in our lives.

The next improvisation is situated in the idea of "teacher in role" (O'Neill, 1995). The teacher (Carmen) takes on a role to engage students in an improvisation that requests the students' presence in another role to engage on a new task. This is the case when Carmen in the role of an advertisement/media representative from an international agency presents to a "selective group of media and advertisement experts" (the students) their new task. They have to prepare a media campaign under the slogan "We are going global" with these artifacts. Carmen presents the goal: Reach an international audience and make these the most successful products in the world. The brief improvisation continues to think through the key factors media experts have to consider in order to sell their products. In this moment, a number of interesting perspectives emerge that relate to the politics of media and the strategic ways media reaches an intended audience. Because we are not media "experts" but we are knowledgeable of media tactics from a consumer's perspective, we imagine and improvise what we think happens behind the scene in the corporate media world. Accuracy does not matter as much in this process; rather what matter are the ways we make visible and reflect on what we know about the politics of media advertising and consumption. This engagement provides a visible place for our awareness to be present in the classroom and to engage in critical scripting performances that are remakes of very complex global dynamics. Finally, we imagine the artifact in the future and write in the role of the artifacts themselves, reflecting on where we ended up, how we got there, and the politics of this trajectory and new location.

Through the construction of multiple improvisational encounters, we (students and Carmen as the facilitator/instructor) find ways to bring some of the global–local naturalized nexus in our lives to construct glocalized consumer literacy pedagogies (Carrington, 2003) as students scripted and rescripted their relationship with the politics of consumption through the artifacts. The artifacts serve as mediators of social, cultural, and political discourses, but it is in the engagement in critical scriptings and performances that these mediations are made visible and acted upon across possible places and temporalities.

PLAYSHOPS AS POSSIBILITIES FOR TEACHER INQUIRY

Playshop (Wohlwend, 2011) is an approach to literacy curriculum and instruction organized around child-led play that encourages pretense to allow children to explore cultural imaginaries of importance to them, such as popular media play worlds and family spheres but also their own imaginaries of schooling. In Chapter 5, Karen described how a kindergarten teacher's imaginative pedagogical practice ruptured a dominant nexus of practice in a neoliberal model of schooling as factory. To do this, Emily, the kindergarten teacher, drew in and improvised on two additional nexus of practice that are widely accepted as educational best practice: (1) developmentally appropriate practice in early childhood education enacted in a model of a nurturing family and (2) process writing practice in elementary education enacted through the model of a reading/writing workshop. We view Emily's intentional use of this convergence as an agentic act of teaching: an invitation to the children to join her teacher-initiated imaginary, *school as playshop*. The curricular model of a playshop blended family and workshop in ways that made literacy personal and available to children and, most relevant here, easily accessed through play. The data examples from Emily's kindergarten in Chapter 5 demonstrate that playshop provided multiple pathways for participating in literacy practices recognized in both peer and school cultures. As a result, children who did not yet read independently in conventional ways could still participate as central players and social leaders in the learning community. This is not always the case for children whose social standing in the classroom is diminished by assumptions about difference and diversity. In many classrooms, marginalization of diverse learners limits their opportunities to develop literacy proficiency. In particular, the factory nexus with a focus on accuracy in decoding and encoding skills and even the workshop nexus with a focus on polishing writerly craft can reduce acceptable literacy performances to a narrow set of written linguistic skills. The playshop works against this to expand who and what is valued.

However, several years after researching this playshop, Karen could locate no other early childhood teachers who were combining play, literacy, and popular media in this way. With the hope of helping other teachers create their own playshops, she began facilitating teacher inquiry groups to help teachers examine the critical and productive learning potential in popular media and to develop play-based and media-rich literacy curriculum.

During one school year, Karen studied with preschool and kindergarten/ first grade teachers in two teacher study groups. Each group met regularly, about every other week, to read research that reconceptualized critical literacy in early childhood education (e.g., Vasquez, 2004), explored young children's play with popular media (e.g., Marsh, 2005a), and media production instructional methods (e.g., Bazalgette, 2010). The teachers had not previously created their own films, so part of the teacher study group time was spent learning filmmaking techniques and planning classroom activities. During the first semester, the teachers acquired skills in filmmaking as they engaged in sample curricular activities such as storyboarding, framing shots, and film editing. However, teachers also shared a number of concerns about popular media that related to expectations in the same three nexus that Emily faced: (1) documenting children's decoding skill to meet teacher accountability and standardized testing expectations in the factory nexus, (2) conferring with children about craft and print expectations in the reading/writing workshop nexus, and (3) meeting expectations for protecting children from problematic media influences in the family nexus.

In the second semester study group sessions, the teachers planned, critiqued, and revised their designed playshop activities; they also responded to student films or short video excerpts of filmmaking activities from their classrooms. Between these sessions, teachers tried out playshop activities with their own students, such as writing scripts, drawing storyboards, animating media toys, making paper puppets, and producing their own films with flip cameras.

Because most media production education has targeted older students, one of the challenges in this work was to locate resources and, importantly, instructional goals that fit and could build upon young children's strengths in dramatic play (Rogow, 2002). For example, the teachers became frustrated in trying to adhere to a prescribed (scripted) linear film production sequence advocated in the media education literature: preproduction scripting and storyboarding, followed by a production phase of rehearsal and final performance, that culminated in a postproduction phase of film editing and special effects. In some ways, the media education books we read circulated expectations that aligned with the factory and workshop models of literacy that emulate adult practices in industry, such as book publishing or film production. For example, sample activities for elementary students were filled with tips for making their films more professional: teaching children to handle and position equipment, using vocabulary with industry terminology, following the pre- to postproduction film design process.

However, after trying media production activities in the readings and noting the high degree of teacher direction and the low degree of student engagement, these early childhood teachers were dissatisfied. Instead, they improvised and found a pathway that made sense within developmentally appropriate discourse and a playshop approach: enabling exploratory play by letting go of the need for a production sequence and instead allowing children to experiment with multiple filmmaking aspects, such as making sound effects, drawing storyboards, recording snippets of dialogue, constructing sets, and playing scenes. Essentially, teachers found that they needed to rupture the workshop process model of film production and adjust their expectations for child-produced films to align with young children's moment-to-moment play goals and fluid storytelling.

Several activities emerged during the school year as key methods for teachers to critically engage the nexus converging in their classrooms and to make tacit expectations visible and amenable to imaginative teaching practices. These activities addressed teachers' interests in developing film knowledge but also connected to our methodology for uncovering, rupturing, and improvising nexus to produce new possibilities for imaginative pedagogies. Two activities illustrate these overlapping analytic tools: playwatching and popular media audits to map the global scope of children's play cultures and analyzing toys and toy commercials to identify scripting and identity texts for opportunities to improvise new ways with toys and media.

Playwatching (Wohlwend et al., 2013) is a specialized form of kidwatching, through which teachers systematically observe children's literacy practices to provide culturally responsive teaching and learning. Contrary to a factory model's interventionist framing that uses teacher observation to locate and remediate learner's skill deficits, teachers use playwatching to actively locate children's assets, such as their attachments to particular media or expertise with global flows, made visible by noticing what children say, do, wear, and play, or noting who plays with whom on the playground. Popular media audits take these observations a step further as teachers research the scope of the reach of the franchises that children bring into their classrooms, similar to the maps of telenovelas and Disney global flows that we created in Chapter 3. Teachers learned about these franchises by browsing cable channel websites, such as PBS or Nick Jr.; locating merchandise on Amazon.com; reading about the franchise narratives, productions, and marketing on Wikipedia; and watching films and television shows. These were not merely academic exercises that demonstrated the immersive and pervasive nature of media flows, but knowledge-generating moves that allowed teachers to discover particular children's expertise and to build bridges in curricular opportunities that allowed children to access their expertise for playgroups (e.g., ideas for character roles or storylines) and for their shared media imaginaries. In addition, playwatching and media audits have potential for rupturing the power relations in adult-dominant nexus of schooling when children are positioned as experts on media unfamiliar to adults or when teachers see how their developmentally appropriate beliefs and attempts to exclude media particularly disadvantages some children. Although well-intentioned, the unintended consequence of prohibiting popular media means that children with the fewest economic resources are least likely to have access to their most familiar toys—and their accompanying linguistic resources. Teachers in the study group faced this rupture when they compared their media audits and suddenly realized that their "commercial-free" stance prohibited children from sharing artifacts of importance in their home, creating a wall rather than the culturally responsive bridges they had advocated. Even though teachers struggled with this rupture, they maintained their rule of prohibiting toys from home throughout the year. None of the teachers allowed children to bring popular media toys to school, although a few teachers provided media toys from *Dora the Explorer* and *Toy Story 3*, franchises they considered acceptable to parents and administrators. In one classroom, children were allowed to play with Disney Princess Barbie dolls, provided by the teachers, for about a month.

The slippages around toys point up the need for teachers to investigate how toys as artifacts bear identity texts and how some toys are constructed within particular nexus as safe while others are not. Nexus analysis (Scollon & Scollon, 2004) of toys and films situates these artifacts in their circulations and histories. In the study group, teachers analyzed a Happy Meal toy as a representative artifact of a popular media franchise, looking at its uses and histories and its play potential. In this critical engagement, we discussed the millions that the media, toy, and fast-food industries spend annually on these cross promotions. The fast-food industry recently spent nearly $294 million on promotions for one year (Marr, 2008). By contrast, we discussed how little educators study what makes popular media so appealing to children. These toys have educational value, problematic when teachers appropriate the toys children love to entice them to complete academic tasks without taking on the additional work of helping children see the messages embedded in these toys or supporting children as they access and play the multiple layers of identities in toys, all with a watchful eye on how players' take up these layers to structure, close off, and open up peer cultures.

Playshops not only provide alternatives to restrictive institutionally given curricula; they also reposition teachers in relation to criticality, media, and young children's peer cultures. Teacher inquiry around playshops moved from critical literacy to critical engagement (Wohlwend & Lewis, 2011) as the target shifted from somewhat heavy-handed problematizing of the identity texts in media toys to supporting children's realization and wielding of these texts within their peer cultures. For example, teachers in Karen's inquiry groups initially aimed to disrupt the gendered stereotypes in identity texts in toys such as Disney Princess dolls. One group attempted to have children sort media toys into girls' toys and boys' toys and then disrupt the resulting binary categories during a group discussion; such critical literacy activities were unsuccessful as children stuck firmly with their original binary categorizations. The early childhood literature is filled with similar failed attempts to raise children's social consciousness about sexism through critical literacy discussions or trade books that trouble their favorite media and familiar stereotypes (e.g., *Paper Bag Princess* by Robert Munsch, 1980). However, when we as an inquiry group looked at the role of popular media toys as markers of belonging (Pugh, 2009), another way forward became visible. Instead of problematizing the widely circulating character and storylines through talk, playshops encourage children to remix and remake the storylines while working within playgroups and filming teams. Teachers then can reposition their mediation; that is, they can encourage players to follow the divergent paths that emerge in play and to explore these possibilities for imagining differently. Additionally, when teachers recognize the passionate attachment that children have to toys (Marsh, 2005a), the ways that children build friendships around their toys (Pugh, 2009; Orenstein, 2011), and the ways identity texts shape inclusion and exclusion in peer culture (Wohlwend, 2005, 2011; Wohlwend et al., 2013), the need for culturally responsive teacher mediation becomes obvious. In this way, critical engagement with gendered toys focuses on how children wield media identity texts with and against one another to structure their social relationships with other children. Imagining differently, then, becomes helping children use media in ways that serve their immediate purposes, expand equitable participation through more inclusive play, and maintain the toys' usefulness for creating friendship bonds in the peer culture.

CONCLUSION

Looking across our work at the intersections of playshop and critical scripting, we see alternatives to prevalent scripted top-down models that provide teachers with fixed strategies. Instead, we see potential for disrupting rigid and predictable pedagogies by embracing the unknowable through improvisation and emergence. In summary, play and performance pedagogies that foreground teachers and children's converging cultural imaginaries provide ways to mediate globalization by:

1. Navigating across multiple sites of engagement and imagined communities to reveal children's and teachers' complex participation in global economies and the uniqueness that emerges as locally situated practices and artifacts.
2. Interrogating participation in connected and expected cultural practices negotiated across sites as nexus of practice, making visible the

relationship between places, temporalities, practices, and participation and focusing on making the everyday "strange."

3. Performing identities through multiliteracies work that strategically uses the ruptures and slippages among converging imaginaries to enable new sites for critical scriptings and playshops to emerge.

In a holistic view of literacy, globalization, and pedagogy as cultural remakings situated in learners' and teachers' complex imaginaries, both curriculum content (or what is constructed through and within play/performance) and instruction (the ways teachers teach, the ways teachers make and frame curricular decisions) mirror each other. That is, what becomes problematic and what has critical potential within children's play and dramatic experiences is what also becomes problematic and has critical potential for reshaping teachers' pedagogies. These mirrorings are opportunities for reflection and recursive reimaginings of what is possible at the intersection of literacy, play, and globalization.

Finally, the work on globalization studies and literacy is emerging, but it is still very small and recent. At this point we feel that we leave this work with as many questions as answers. As we said in the introduction, we hope to invite readers to reflect, explore, and continue this conversation. What we share here are ongoing projects that trigger new and old possibilities in the ways we envision the role of literacy, play, and dramatic experiences as cultural production.

Appendix A

Competing over *Aladdin and the King of Thieves* and a Whole CD Pack[1]

Stephen: Gavin! Gavin! Have you watched, um, *Aladdin, King of Thieves*?
Stephen: There's a song about [*singing*] "There's a party here in Africa." [*waving one hand with raisin above his head in a circling motion*]
Gavin: I know.
Stephen: You heard, uh, you watched it! *Aladdin, King of Thieves*?
Gavin: Yeah.
Stephen: That's me too! I watched it at my Grandma's.
Sasha: What about—did you watch—about in Abraguuh
Stephen: Well, we did. At my Grandma's.
Sasha: What about Aladdin of Jasmine?
Stephen: [*to Justin*] Did you watch, umm, *Aladdin, King of Thieves*? There's a song about [*singing*] "There's a party here in Africa."
Justin: No, Africa's not.
Stephen: [*disagreeing with Justin*] I hearrd.
Gavin: [*agreeing with Stephen*] And me. Okay, this is slippery [*trying to open box of raisins*]
Justin: [*to Gavin*] Hey, guess what?
Gavin: [*singing*] "There's a party here in Africa."
Sasha: Abriga
Stephen: [*noticing his own error in pronunciation*] ABRIGah, not Africa. Abrigah.
Sasha: [*to Stephen, correcting his pronunciation*] AbregUH, GUH
Stephen: Abriguh, Abriguh
Sasha: [*nods head to approve pronunciation*]
Stephen: Can you open that? [*indicating Fruit Roll-Up in plastic wrap*]
Justin: [*to Callie across the table*] I have a whole CD pack at home. A whole CD pack. [*adding emphasis with a wave of his arm*] A whole CD pack. Can you believe that?
Callie: No wonder.
Stephen: [*to Callie*] Callie, did you watch *Aladdin, King of Thieves*? There's a song about [*singing*] "There's a party here in Afriguh. We all know we can't wait."

Justin: [*leaning across table to address Gavin*] Hey, guess what? I have a whole CD pack at home. A whole CD pack. Can you believe that? A whole CD pack. But not Aladdin [*turning away from Stephen*] CD. It's wap. [louder]

Justin: [*after no response from Gavin, repeats*] It's wap.

Sasha: [*singing*] "There's a party here in Abrigah."

Callie: [to Justin] How many do you have?

Sasha: [*singing*] "We almost can't wait. There's a party here in Abrigah."

Justin: [to Callie] 19. 19. Like 19. I have 19.

Callie: [to Justin] Well I have that other one.

Justin: [to Callie]: I have, I like have, I have 16. I have like 16 CDs. I even got a pack for my birthday. I got two CDs for my birthday and a radio. And a holder. For my birthday.

Callie: He got two.

Justin: I got all of that for my birthday. Can you believe it? And fish. Two fish.

Stephen: I got a hundred of 'em.

Justin: No. Really. REALLY. I got fish for my birthday and a radio and two CDs and a holder for 'em.

Stephen: [simultaneously] A hundred of 'em.

Callie: [to Justin] Keep talkin' keep talkin' keep talkin'.

Justin: I had my name all over it. I writed my name all over it.

Stephen: A hundred of 'em.

A few minutes later, there is a brief argument over whether Justin actually knows who Jafar is.

Stephen: [*stands up to enact a pose as Jafar the villain from* Aladdin]

Justin: I HAVE Aladdin.

Stephen: You don't have *Aladdin Jafar Part II*.

Justin: [*looks at Callie, blinking in an exaggerated way while slapping his own head repeatedly—a move reminiscent of Three Stooges slapstick*]

Appendix B

Originally received by Editorial Office, August 14, 2010; Sent to T&F, July 1, 2012

MEDIA AS NEXUS OF PRACTICE: REMAKING IDENTITIES IN *WHAT NOT TO WEAR*

Karen E. Wohlwend* and Carmen L. Medina

In this conceptual piece, we examine media as a nexus of a traditional schooling pedagogy and performance pedagogy to make visible how their overlapping elements produce media's pervasive educative force but also to gain a deeper understanding of the complexities of using media in educational contexts. Nexus analysis examines a fashion makeover television program—*What Not to Wear*—as an embodied lesson that produces identity revision but also disjunctures and slippages that enable critical responses and productive remakings. WNTW is a dramatization of remediation of one woman's (portrayed) lived practices and clothing choices that are read on her body as personal expression of fashion trends. These globalized lessons with body texts require new ways of reading and responding that allow learners/viewers to see the power relations that construct particular identity performances as errors and cultural practices and ethnicities as unacceptable.

Keywords: Gender, globalization, critical media curricula, identity revision, performance pedagogy, mediated discourse analysis

Through global networks and round-the-clock broadcasting, media reach audiences around the world through popular television programs, films,

* Corresponding author: Literacy, Culture, and Language Education, School of Education, Indiana University, 3042 Wright Education Building, Bloomington, IN 47405, U.S. Email: kwohlwen@indiana.edu.

video games, consumer products, and advertising (Appadurai, 1996; Maira & Soep, 2005; Rantane, 2004). In response to the pervasive presence of media texts, teachers are urged to enliven school curricula by making room for and making use of students' popular media knowledge and passions. We see at least two takes on the role of media education in schools: a critical pedagogy framing of media that addresses hegemony and power in relation to the material effects of media representation (Giroux & McClaren, 1994; Macedo & Gounari, 2005; Macedo & Steinberg, 2007; McClaren, 1995; Duncan-Andrade & Morrell, 2007) and a post-structural feminist stance that considers dispersed power, agentic action on the part of consumer/producers, and takes a complicated view of identity and representation (Ellsworth, 2005; Marshall & Sensoy, 2011). In our literacy teaching and research, we advocate critical media curricula that fuses popular media, creative production, and critical perspectives (Buckingham, 2003), often finding ourselves teaching with and against media in complicated ways.

Whether or not teachers intentionally incorporate television and film texts into curricula, we argue that popular media are already there, omnipresent pedagogies that powerfully shape who we can be and how we can act within classrooms and communities (Ellsworth, 2005; Kellner & Share, 2005; Medina, 2001, 2010; Wohlwend, 2009a, 2009c). In this paper, we use mediated discourse analysis to make sense of the overlapping practices and pedagogies in critical media education, looking closely at the ways performance pedagogy creates alternatives and possibilities for productive and critical response.

Popular media texts that excite students' interest also circulate idealized expectations, exaggerated gender models, and problematic racial and ethnic representations. For example, popular media messages affect girls' self-image with implications for their academic trajectories and future lives (Mazzarella & Pecora, 2002).

> Issues of identity and body image are foregrounded in such a way that a girl's identity is intricately linked to her physical appearance and compliant behavior. Mainstream culture, found in messages in school as well as out-of-school contexts, "instructs" girls on the "approved" ways to become women. Pipher (1994) referred to a "girl-poisoning culture" (p. 20) and demonstrated that girls seem to lose themselves in adolescence, and they know it. (Sanford, 2005, p. 305)

Others have argued that media act as a cultural pedagogy that masks its individuating and regulating gaze as well as its ability to deflect attention from itself (Kellner & Share, 2005). Often, "it is women's bodies that are the problem rather than the institutionalized scripts through which girls are socialized into gendered identities" (Marshall & Sensoy, 2009, p. 160). Further, postfeminism circulates a vision of perpetual self-improvement that focuses attention on beauty ideals that work to:

re-secure the terms of submission of white femininity to white masculine domination, while simultaneously resurrecting racial divisions
by undoing any promise of multi-culturalism through the exclusion of
non-white femininities from this rigid repertoire of selfstyling. (McRobbie, 2009, p. 70)

We argue that one among the many ways popular media work as a powerful
pedagogy relates to the emerging spaces constructed between performance
practices and more traditional views of pedagogy. These intersections are evident in popular "lifestyle television" programming (Hollows, 2000), where
actors and audiences engage in the process of educating and being educated
on particular lifestyles that are meant to develop ideal identities. "Lifestyle
programming in all its forms operates on [an] assumption—that all goods
(clothes, kitchens, and backyards) function as signs of identity—they tell others who we are (or rather who we want to be)" (Palmer, 2004, p. 178).

In this conceptual piece, we work around the question: How do popular
media function as a pedagogy situated in the nexus of educative and dramatized practices? *What Not to Wear* (WNTW) is an example of reality
television that has a particularly direct model of education. We noticed
the connections to education (explicit instruction of "the rules", models,
guided practice) in our own viewing and believed a close look at this program could be useful in triggering new ways of looking at reality television
across ages, including programs about young children, such as *Nanny 911*,
or for adolescents, such as MTV's *Teen Mom*. Perhaps more important, we
believe such analysis also has potential to complicate current understandings of performative identity work in schools. We look closely at one lifestyle television program, WNTW,[1] to tease out its pedagogical elements and
the disjunctures and slippages that enable critical response and remakings.
WNTW is a fashion makeover, a highly popular self- and home-improvement genre of television shows, evident in cable programming filled with
similar shows such as *10 Years Younger*, *Trading Spaces*, *Save My Bath*,
Rate This Space, and *Date My House*. Self- and home-improvement are the
goals of makeover television. In the case of WNTW, participants learn to
dress more fashionably through intensive lessons in clothing selection, hair
styling, and cosmetics application. Each WNTW episode follows a predictable before-and-after sequence as "fashion experts" critique and correct
the "style" of a surprised subject, usually a woman, who has been identified
as a "fashion disaster" by her relatives and friends (WNTW, 2009).

In this article, we take a step back to critically read one WNTW episode as a disciplinary lesson that instructs distant viewers how to consume and which goods are necessary for desirable identity performances
of mainstream femininity. We see potential in this nexus of pedagogies as
a contested and transformative space dense with opportunities for individuals to improvise and productively use power. We analyze excerpts from
one WNTW episode to explore how a fashion makeover functions (1) as

a school-like lesson that reinscribes a mainstream set of fashion norms for gender and ethnicity performances, and (2) as a playful, dramatized performance with pedagogical elements that challenge identity erasure and proliferate available ways of being.

NEXUS OF PRACTICE

Identity performances, including those scrutinized and remade in WNTW episodes, are situated in *nexus of practice* (Scollon, 2001), networks of implicit, valued practices and expectations that mark membership. Nexus are "sites of engagement" where multimodal interaction, social practices, histories for use of materials, and discourses that circulate in a particular place "come together to form an action in real time" (p. 28). In the current analysis, it is important to consider how nexus not only serve as markers of membership in the imagined community of fashionable women but also how nexus circulate cultural ideals, teach membership expectations, and recruit participants. In WNTW, the formulaic scenes and repetitive practices centre on correcting the participant's use of key fashion practices (wearing particular combinations of clothing articles, selecting event-appropriate outfits) in order to inscribe the identity *worst dressed*. During each episode, normally tacit practices are foregrounded for the individual (and viewers) and explicitly taught in ways that make visible the range of acceptable and unacceptable identity performances. As the show's subject stands in front of the mirror, the hosts read her reflected image for its cultural value, specifically, its congruence with postfeminist beauty ideals circulating in popular media. As the title of the show suggests, these readings are intentionally negative, focusing on "outdated" clothing that women should not wear and should not *want* to wear (Wohlwend, 2009c, p. 73).

We examine how this fashion makeover program teaches participants and viewers to value dominant gender and ethnicity performances through negative fashion readings of (primarily) women's bodies, accompanied by a performative pedagogy that enabled moving between spaces and ruptures. We argue that WNTW operates through media pedagogies through a range of familiar practices and scripts. The makeover genre circulates a foregrounded self-improvement pedagogy to educate viewers about better ways of living with newer possessions (Palmer, 2004). For example, as self-improvement pedagogy, this "how-to" television genre simulates remedial teaching with individualized prescription and correction. Each television episode acts as a lesson that teaches viewers to improve their lifestyle practices through demonstrations of new ways of decorating homes, cooking meals, or dressing bodies.

A makeover program circulates and is produced through practices of backgrounded performance pedagogies that produce dramatized examples and counterexamples of cultural values. From the perspective of performance pedagogy, each episode is a production, a how-to dramatization that shows viewers how to perform a credible identity as a sexualized subject who fully participates in postfeminist consumer culture. In WNTW, media pedagogies emphasize female consumers' obligation to "stay current" by wearing new styles that require the latest mainstream-sanctioned products and necessitate purchases of up-to-date consumer goods and services.

> A sizable proportion of lifestyle television is devoted to the stigmatization of those who are laggardly or recalcitrant in their fulfillment of this duty and, through a combination of public shaming and financial incentives, to inducing them to become fully participant, consuming subjects in the neoliberal economy. (Roberts, 2007, p. 228)

In each WNTW episode, a sequence of critiques and demonstrations teaches the targeted person—"contributor"—who has been identified as a "walking fashion disaster" to purchase and coordinate articles of clothing in acceptable combinations. Each contributor is transformed over the course of one episode as she trades in her old wardrobe for a $5000 shopping trip. The show follows a formulaic progression of scenes: initial confrontation, explicit instruction in proper dressing, independent and guided shopping practice, hair and makeup demonstrations, and final product/performance evaluation by experts. The key scenes and repetitive practices centre on correcting the subject's purported misuse of key backgrounded practices and preferences for objects of distaste (e.g., clothes, shoes, makeup outside current fashion trends). These practices are foregrounded in the show and explicitly taught in ways that revise novices' identity performances according to postfeminist fashion rules and cultural models. The dramatized and edited excerpts in WNTW provide vivid examples of identity revision, making this fashion makeover program an apt choice for illustrating how backgrounded nexus of practice and foregrounded correction of mediated actions constitute identity revision that powerfully influences opportunities to learn and participate in imagined communities (including classrooms).

Media, like all forms of performance including play, almost always involve representations and transformations of identity. The makeover genre makes this explicit in its demand for identity revision according to a set of stated and unstated norms; in this case, fashion norms in a complicated mix of discourses about femininity. Women are the target audience for makeover television; the genre circulates a discourse of postfeminism that constructs women as empowered, sexualized subjects who consume fashion and transform their bodies in order to please themselves, not men (Gill, 2007). How does WNTW teach audiences who they should be and what displays of body count as appropriate performances necessary for belonging in an imagined community of fashionable women?

CORRECTIVE PEDAGOGIES

In a prescription and correction model of learning, learners are expected to follow instructor directions during discrete direct instruction lessons and complete tasks in conventionally accurate ways. Such lessons follow formulaic designs (Hunter, 1982):

1. Objectives
2. Standards
3. Anticipatory set
4. Teaching (input, modeling, check for understanding)
5. Guided practice/monitoring/re-teaching
6. Closure
7. Independent practice

In such lessons, corrective pedagogies require instructors to deliver content, model skills, and provide guided practice that is carefully monitored for deficits that are remediated through re-teaching. This approach enables testing and ranking of students according to the degree to which their skill performances adhere to mainstream norms. Media makeovers employ similar practices that promote uniform application of content, consistent with a skills mastery discourse (Ivanič, 2004) that circulates through government mandates for accountability and standardization (NCLB, 2002).

PERFORMANCE PEDAGOGIES

A significant element of popular media relates to how media work as performance pedagogies (Conquergood, 1998; Garoian, 1999; Pineau, 2002). Performance arts and pedagogies intersect to "represent an expanded, heterogeneous field of cultural work within which the body performs various aspects of production, socially and historically constructed behaviors that are learned and reproduced" (Garoian, 1999, p. 8). Performance pedagogies provide a view of identity in contemporary media that contests more traditional views of production and identity representations as finalized, rehearsed, and fixed. It emphasizes the flux of productivity as well as its product. As feminist performance theorist Diamond suggests, performance is always "a doing and a thing done" where:

> even its dazzling physical immediacy, drifts between present and past, presence and absence, consciousness and memory. Every performance, if it is intelligible as such, embeds features of previous performances: gender conventions, racial histories, aesthetic traditions—political and cultural pressures, that are consciously and unconsciously acknowledged. (1996, p. 1)

A view of media as performance pedagogies helps us understand how embodying particular identities works at the core of the production of a television show and how identities are produced, reproduced, resisted, and transformed as people "learn" new cultural practices. In media make-overs, performance actors and audiences are engaged in "improvisational encounters" where the production of identity is embedded in complex dynamics "playing" multiple positionings that are simultaneously situated between the real, the fictional, and the social. These positionings are in many instances in tension with each other, resulting in hybrid spaces where actual and projected identities are perceived in relation to ways of living and participating in communities including racial, ethnic, and gender positionings.

Notions of embodiment constitute key elements of how performance pedagogies are understood, particularly in feminist poststructuralist (Davies, 1993; Grosz, 1994; Pillow, 2003; St. Pierre & Pillow, 2000) and feminist performance theories (Diamond, 1996; Garoian, 1999; Patraka, 1999; Phelan, 1993; Pineau, 2002). Embodiment—"the body's social text" (Diamond, 1996, p. 4)—and the reinscription of bodies are also at the core of how makeover television works, particularly in shows like WNTW. Somerville (2004) suggests that "the body can intervene in discourse just as discourse can intervene into the body" (p. 51). In this dynamic, bodies are perceived as texts that simultaneously inscribe and are inscribed by social discourses. The conceptualization of what embodiment has to offer is not understood just in material and biological terms but in more expansive ways to consider the body as a site of social, political, and cultural inscription (Perry & Medina, 2011). In our view of the role of performance and embodiment in WNTW, we perceive a productive tension between how bodies are disciplined (Foucault, 1995) and the forms of resistance that are made visible by the participants in the show.

Based on the above framework we identified two elements that are helpful here in looking at popular media as performance pedagogies:

1. Embodied texts—bodies write and are written through cultural symbols and practices.
2. Productivity of improvisations vs. production of dramatic events. In improvisation, identities are fluid and dynamic and not rehearsed and fixed.

MEDIATED DISCOURSE ANALYSIS

Recursive processes of data collection and analysis in mediated discourse analysis provide a systematic way to look closely at the way that even the smallest ways with things—glancing at another's paper, holding a pencil just so—fulfill embodied expectations for particular identities within a nexus of practice. For example, teachers may closely observe students' mediated actions to identify learners for remedial teaching (Wohlwend, 2009b), teaching that often involves practicing particular mediated actions until they become automatic (e.g., touching words on a page, printing on a line) and can be instantly recognized as student performances of literate identities (Luke, 1992).

Mediated discourse analysis focuses on mediated actions—physical actions with material objects—to understand how nonverbal actions in everyday, taken-for-granted practices accept and evoke some identities but not others according to nexus of practice, a mesh of embodied expectations collectively set and reset through shared histories. Specifically, mediated discourse analysis uncovers how physical mediated actions interact to constitute social practices, how social practices interact in local contexts, and how nexus of locally valued practices build identities and meanings situated in power relations circulated through global discourses.

Mediated discourse analysis sifts data to identify the key players, scenes, valued practices, and transformative events, making visible how practices and pedagogies mesh to teach preferred identity performances (e.g., *lifestyles*). Through a funnel design, mediated discourse analysis filters data to locate particular events in which nexus of key practices transform identities. Table B.1 shows the progression of analysis where the first step, Locating Participants and Means (row 1), locates participants' concerns and identifies the means of circulating relevant discourses, in this case women and a postfeminist interest in fashionable dressing depicted in makeover television.

The second step, Observing Scenes and Practices (row 2), identifies the recurring kinds of scenes, such as critiques such as the initial confrontation, secret video, or 360 mirror critiques or demonstrations such as the presentation of properly attired mannequins that are key parts of the WNTW makeover formula. In this article we focus on the third step and fourth steps.

The third step, Locating Nexus of Practice (row 3), examines scenes within the progression of a single episode, to see how practices work together as nexus to circulate valued ways of belonging. In WNTW, the nexus of corrective and performative practices for evaluating and displaying clothing and bodies come together repeatedly across critique scenes in the episode with Cristina, a Latina drama teacher, to construct her as a remedial subject. The most significant and engrained practices in nexus circulate power, recruit members, and enforce identity-building activity (Gee, 1999), in this case correcting the ways that errant members (the worst dressed) choose and use cultural artifacts (clothing) in order to instruct female viewers how to construct selves with fashion.

In the fourth step, Locating Transformative Episodes (row 4), moments of transformation are located in the progression of critique scenes, in this case, places where identity shifts occur, as Cristina works with and against corrective and performative practices to perform multiple roles.

In the fifth step, Microanalysis of Mediated Actions (row 5), key moments of identity change are examined through microanalysis that looks closely at interaction (physical actions as well as language) for immediate transformational effects but also for links to global systems and discourses. In this conceptual piece, we do not attempt a full mediated discourse analysis but merely suggest the explanatory potential of the concept of nexus of practice for understanding complicated and contradictory media messages.

Table B.1   Research Filters in Mediated Discourse Analysis with WNTW Examples

Research Filters	Unit of Analysis	Looking for	WNTW Examples
1. Locating Participants and Means	Locations	Participants and their concerns	Women and fashionable dress
		Social issues	Feminine ideal
		Means and media	Fashion, television, and makeover genre
		Discourses	Postfeminism
2. Observing Scenes and Practices	Scenes	Patterns of valued practices in recurring scenes across formulaic episodes	Recurring critique scenes: Trash can scene / Shopping critique scene
3. Locating Nexus of Practice	Linked practices	Nexus where overlapping practices intensify social effects	Evaluating clothes (subject), relinquishing preferred garments, accepting surveillance, correcting error, promoting self-scrutinizing subject
4. Locating Transformative Episodes	Progression within a particular episode	Transformation: cultural capital, symbolic violence	From defense of favorite outfit to acceptance of unfashionable self and need for correction
5. Microanalysis of Mediated Actions	Mediated action	Construction of relational identities and social spaces	Construction of fashion error, need for expert remediation, hosts as fashion experts, media as instructional space

TEACHING IDENTITY IN MEDIA NEXUS OF PRACTICE

We examine media as a nexus of practice situated in overlapping pedagogies to make visible how combined pedagogies produce media's pervasive educative force but also to gain a deeper understanding of the complexities of using media in educational contexts. Table B.2 represents our analysis of WNTW within this nexus of practice. In this article, we analyze excerpts from this episode to understand how the "trash can scene" used school pedagogy elements to discipline and inscribe embodied texts and how performance pedagogy amplified resistant performances.

Table B.2   Negotiated Practices in Corrective and Performance Pedagogies in WNTW Scenes

WNTW Scene	*A Corrective Pedagogy: Practices in a Lesson*	*A Performance Pedagogy: Practices in Improvisation*	*Coproduction: Negotiated Practices*
Critique Scenes: Secret Video, *Trash Can,* Mirror scenes	Establish need State objectives	Contested space Resistant performance	Discipline in assessment of needs Inscribing texts through projected identities
Rules and Models: Fashion rules presented on mannequins	Model skill or concept: presenting standards, teaching modeling	Imagined final product Projected dominant identities	Production of (possible) embodied texts through modeling
Shopping Trip 1, solo with critique at close of day	Independent practice Check for understanding	Producing Rehearsing	Attempting and assimilating the given embodied text
Shopping Trip 2, with "surprise" appearance by hosts and guided shopping	Guided practice Monitoring Assessment and feedback Reteaching through guided practice	Proliferating identities through improvisation creative generation of embodied texts	Imposing, improvising, and appropriating identities in between present and past, presence and absence, consciousness and memory
Final Reveal: Homecoming	Closure and final evaluation	Performing in the lines	Mastering skills and disciplined bodies Display of emergent embodied texts

Note: Italic font indicates the scenes analyzed in this article.

EDUCATING CRISTINA, THE "MOST DIFFICULT CONTRIBUTOR"

To understand how the show teaches identity performances in complicated ways, we examine excerpts from an episode featuring a Puerto Rican drama teacher, described by one of the hosts as the "most difficult contributor ever" to appear on the show. The aim of WNTW is to explicitly teach the contributor, or featured participant, to identify valued ways of dressing to fit the postfeminist ideal of a successful, modern woman. But what do participants actually contribute? Ostensibly their wardrobes, but in effect, contributors submit their bodies and identity performances for reading and correction.

Trash can scene:
Constructing need, performing resistance, and disciplining Cristina

Cristina: That is a great piece.
[Stacey grimaces and tosses the lace top into trash can.]

Cristina: You know, I want to jump in there *[Points to the trash can.]*
I need a therapist.
[Both hosts place hands on hips, and Clinton rolls his eyes.]

Stacey: This is the therapy, baby. Get used to it.

Cristina: Help!
[She shakes bar of clothes rack as if shaking the bars of a cage.]

Stacey: Oh, yeah. Help is right. Help.
[Stacey continues to rummage through the clothing on rack.]
Help! Help us! *[Mocking Cristina]*

Cristina: No puedo, no puedo, no puedo.
[Clinton shuts his eyes while Stacey gasps and opens mouth in exaggerated shock and surprise at Cristina's shift to Spanish.]
[Cristina continues in Spanish, using Spanish to express emotion and shut out hosts. As Cristina speaks, she gestures to her breasts.] They're not happy.

Stacey: Oy.

Clinton: I don't know what she said but she . . .
[Changes pitch to enact a whining childish voice] . . . sounded mad.
[Stacey echoes Clinton's enactment—also assumes a crying tone]
I know.

Cristina: That's Cristina . . . *[Gesturing to clothes in trash can]*
              . . . that you're throwing out. I have nothing left.
              [Gestures to torso in circular motion.]

Cristina: *[Switching to a calm voice and composed stance, clasping hands.]*
              You know what? I think you guys should go, you did a great job,
              thank you, and I'll take care of this.
              *[Cristina firmly grasps the trash can with the overflowing pile
              of clothes.]*
Clinton: Oh thanks. You're excusing us? You're the boss? Cristina:
              Well, no. I just don't want you guys to work any harder.
Stacy: *[Points with entire arm.]*
              You know what? You. Out. Go shopping.
Clinton: Yeah. Out. Go shopping. Bye. Stacey: Remember, the rules.
              *[Cristina grasps the sides of the trash can mounded over with
              her clothes and begins dragging it out of the studio, clothes spill-
              ing out along the way.]*

Clinton: *[Shouting]* Cristina! We're going to call the authorities.
              *[Cristina screams as Stacey tips over the trash can, dumps the
              clothes on the floor. Stacey strikes bodybuilder pose.]*

Clinton: *[To Cristina]* Look what you've done. You've made a mess.

Cristina: Oh-uh-uh-uh-uh *[exaggerated sobbing sounds.]* You've destroyed
              me. You've destroyed me. It's over. *[Drops article of clothing.]*
              You know what. I have no soul. Cristina? That's Cristina for you.
              [Indicating discarded clothing].
              This? *[Indicating body]* I have no idea who this is.

WNTW makes the boundaries of a fashionable lifestyle explicit through
negative examples that point out individual fashion blunders. What "we"
hate is made explicit through individuated exemplars and their articles of
clothing become markers that reinforce the boundaries (Wilk, 2000). In
this way, WNTW polices the border of fashionable dressing. Attractive-
ness is the overriding criterion as hosts ignore or ridicule contributors'
reasons for keeping articles of clothing that don't follow the rules: a
treasured sweater from a loved one, a pair of practical shoes for work,
a cheaper dress that fits a family's economic realities, or objects that are
physically or emotionally comforting. Ethnicity is never addressed or
acknowledged as a valid concern on the program. However, Woodward
(2007) found that clothing choices not only represent but construct identities, producing daily anxieties about appearing "not me" while working through:

the contradictions and ambivalences which are core to women's clothing choices. Irrespective of women's social positioning or background,
the pivotal dynamic which underpins how women choose what to wear
is between clothing that is "easy" and "safe," and clothing that allows
women to transform themselves. (2007, p. 340)

In this early scene in the episode, Cristina resists the hosts' trashing of her
wardrobe, explicitly framing the critique as erasure. She describes the identity
work as an assault, "You've destroyed me. It's over. You know what, I have
no soul," inscribing her body as a text to respond to the symbolic violence
in the somewhat physical confrontation. Cristina's attempts to reclaim her
wardrobe demonstrate her resistance to trashing her identity, which she will
eventually call "the old Cristina." Her actions can be read as moves to leave
an unbearable situation in order to escape identity erasure, and the hosts'
violent reactions can be read as countermoves to block her escape. Cristina is
valuable as the object of the show; she serves as a bad example, an unfashion-
able subject. This video clip reveals the violence in identity revision in structured pedagogy of schooling. The interaction indexes corporal punishment
in the physical restraint and the host/teacher's demonstration of power as she
tips over the trash can and blames the contributor/student for making a mess.
Because the media scene occurs in a drama/schooling nexus, the symbolic
and material violence to identities in structured pedagogy is exaggerated and
made visible through the combination of the embodying and dramatizing
pedagogy of dramatic performance. The hosts' clowning entertains audiences
and frames their critique as playful teasing.

> This is popular entertainment which uses irony to suggest that it is not
> meant to be taken literally. However, this does not mean that there is
> no humiliation. Participants frequently dissolve into tears and there
> is "panic mingled with revolt" as they are put through their paces,
> unlearning what is considered unacceptable and unattractive about
> themselves. (McRobbie, 2004, p. 105)

We also see productivity in this scene as Cristina improvises and performs
in and out of several identities. We see her drawing upon cultural repertoires (Gutiérrez & Rogoff, 2003) of teaching, drama, and ethnicities to
perform resistance through fluid moment-to-moment changes in roles as
Cristina as defiant Latina, Cristina as teacher in charge, and Cristina as
considerate and compliant contributor.

Playing past compliance/resistance

Second shopping trip scene:
Reteaching skills, improvising roles, and proliferating identities

Cristina: So you see, Clinton? Low-cut, see-through, hmmmm.
[*Holds black dress up and sways as she sings*]
"You say good-bye, I say hello . . ."
[*Waits for response from hosts*]
Uh-huh.
[*Hosts look at each other and roll their eyes.*]

Cristina: [*Holding up second dress*]
This is something I would wear . . . right before I jumped off a bridge. And you can see me going—Aaaaaahhhh
[*Waving her arm to indicate slow-motion falling*]
and you can see the dress going
[*Whistles and billows out dress to simulate falling*]
[*Hosts burst out laughing and continue to struggle to resume their mock severity as Cristina picks out a third dress, exclaiming*]
Ooooh.

Clinton: Why don't you show us some things that follow the rules that we showed you?

Cristina: I don't remember the rules. I was too traumatized.
[*Cristina chooses a fourth dress and holds up the dress with hanger behind her neck.*]

Clinton: The only way you're walking out with that in your hands is stepping over my lifeless body.
[*Cristina removes dress from her neck.*]
Guys, you have to have a little room to be crazy. I mean everything is not like . . .
[*Holds dress stiffly in front of her and marches in small circle.*]

Clinton: You've got more than a little room. Our body parts don't talk to us . . . or at least not that we're willing to admit.

Cristina: You need to be in tune with your body.
[*Both hosts burst out laughing and Cristina scolds*]
Look at you, having a great time at my expense, huh.

Stacey: Absolutely not at your expense, Cristina.
[*Laughing and smirking.*]

Cristina: I'll try on what you suggested.
[*Walks off stiffly with arms extended out in front of her.*]

In this scene, we see elements of corrective pedagogy as Cristina as the "off-task" student, playing the clown, thwarting the teachers when she should be applying previous lessons to her remedial practice. However, in this instance, Cristina foregrounds the stage and uses the tool of improvisation in performance pedagogy to morph rapidly through roles, seductive temptress who sings to Clinton, suicidal fashion victim who jumps off a bridge, traumatized student who can't remember the "rules," and the robotic soldier who complies with orders. In response, the hosts use the stage to mock Cristina's performances and her admonition to be "in tune with your body" by joking about how she talks for and with her body ("they are unhappy"). Of course, performance pedagogy provides deniability for these jabs as it's just a performance, all for the entertainment of viewers at home.

MAKEOVERS AS EMBODIED, DRAMATIZED, AND GLOBALIZED LESSONS

It is important to remember that Cristina is not the only one who learns. Drama is a spatialized and spatializing literacy that allows Cristina's embodied lesson to reach wide audiences with viewers as remote learners and the studio as an imagined classroom. Each distant learner is tacitly invited to view herself along with the foregrounded subject (for studies on media audience and reception, see Hall, 1992; Lull, 1990; and Morley, 1986). Viewers also learn to contribute; they read their own bodies and they revise their own identity performances to comply with the self-help advice and to participate in the discourses of postfeminism. This goal is apparent in Cristina's episode as she talks about her successful search for an idealized, essentialized, and unified identity, an improved self through the fashion makeover: "Not only did I find Cristina, but I found a new Cristina."

The show's pedagogy teaches viewers to critique others as well as themselves. Fans can demonstrate their ability to recognize others who do not know "what not to wear" through the device of peer nominations. On the program website, viewers are invited to nominate friends and family members as future participants. The nomination also establishes the nominator as a fashion-wise member of an imagined community of stylish women. As fans watch WNTW's cautionary tales, they learn to apply the lessons to read bodies and revise identity performances:

- To read their bodies and clothing practices as lacking (need)
- To monitor their own fashion errors, as well as others (surveillance)
- To recognize, value, and seek out expert advice for identity revision (compliance)
- To take up new fashion practices that circulate an imperative to consume (regeneration)

A further step back reveals that the show's intensive critique and insistence on compliance with beauty ideals reiterates, week after week, that women and girls must attend to physical presentation of self through proper bodily displays.

Thus, this television makeover program operates as an embodied lesson on (at least) two planes. First, the program is a dramatization that represents one woman's (portrayal of) lived practices and clothing choices that are read on her body as personal expression of fashion trends. Second, each videotaped episode in the reality program is a globalized lesson, situated in the nexus of discourses about gender, ethnicity, and consumerism that shape viewer identities. These media lessons with body texts require new ways of reading and responding that allow learners to see the power relations behind constructions of identity performances as errors and cultural practices as unacceptable.

PERFORMANCE AS PRODUCTIVE CRITICAL RESPONSE TO MEDIA PEDAGOGIES

This examination of a media makeover demonstrates, perhaps not surprisingly, that media are not innocent; media circulate and legitimate powerful discourses and dominant cultural models, in this instance those associated with corrective pedagogies. However, the juxtaposition with performance pedagogies provides opportunities for micro tactics (Foucault, 1978). On first reading, we saw reproduction of stereotypical roles along with Cristina's resistance. But when we looked more closely, we saw agency and productivity in the fluidity of her playful proliferation of identities. Reading Cristina's response as resistance or rupture is too narrow, too unidirectional, relying on dualistic notions of power and identity. Rather, we see her dramatized critique as divergent tangles of multiple, complicated, and complicating performances.

As educators, we need critical readings and responses that deconstruct and disrupt, yet embrace media texts and provide multiple paths in, out, and around its powerful discourses. Performance pedagogies provide improvisational space that brings implicit discourses up to the surface, making the tacit visible and accessible for deconstruction. We see media as the site of many overlapping nexus that can integrate or clash. As Baker and Green (2007) suggest, we might "turn this 'frame clash' into what Agar (2004, p. 21) calls a 'rich point,' a point where cultural patterns, practices, and knowledge become visible" (p. 194).

IMPLICATIONS: TEACHING WITH AND AGAINST MEDIA

Of course, each episode is an explicitly dramatized staged performance and not an accurate representation of lived experience. And contrary to the "happy ending" constructed in each episode, we don't know if contributors' lives are enhanced, harmed, or unchanged by their participation in the show. However, these concerns are largely beside the point. The relationship between staging the performance of everyday life and the everyday life serving as a staged performance is a provocative element of new media for viewers engaged in the consumption of these shows. In WNTW, the real learners are television viewers who learn to avoid fashion errors through teaching that corrects by ridiculing and amplifying errors so consumers can see what *not* to do. This makeover exemplifies how media nexus brings together the immersive and transformative power of dramatized texts and pervasive schooling of selves through media. When we teach with media, we're inviting a powerful, very effective teacher into our classrooms. This suggests that rather than treating media as a textual object, we should be treating media as rich sites of identity play and embodied production, more amenable to immersive performance pedagogies than detached rational deconstructions (Medina & Wohlwend, in press). We will require more than the traditional tools of critical literacy, of literature discussion that deconstructs, responds, and sometimes redesigns. We will need performative pedagogies that let us try on uncomfortable identities, look critically at ourselves clothed in roles we hate, and play our way out of trouble.

Notes

NOTES TO CHAPTER 2

1. The structured analysis of identities as discrete entities should be viewed as a useful heuristic rather than a representation of actual lived lives. Individuals enact heteroglossic (Bakhtin, 1981) identity performances that draw upon and link shared histories of social relationships and classroom power relations.

NOTES TO CHAPTER 3

1. There are two Disney Princess characters, Anna and Elsa, in the latest film, *Frozen*.

NOTES TO CHAPTER 4

1. All names are pseudonyms.

NOTES TO CHAPTER 5

1. All names are pseudonyms.
2. Mary Poppins is the titular character in a live-action Disney film. While not a Disney Princess, the children sometimes included the magical governess in their improvisations on family and princess narratives.

NOTES TO APPENDIX A

1. Transcription conventions

[ ]	Actions or modes (gesture, handling objects, gaze, sound effects, changes in speech: pitch, quality)
repeated letter	Stretched phoneme
CAPITALS	Noticeably louder than surrounding words
space	Pause

NOTES TO APPENDIX B

1. *What Not to Wear* is a reality show that originated in the UK; the scenes featured here are excerpted from the U.S. version, which airs on The Learning Channel cable network.

References

Aaker, D. A. (1996). *Building strong brands*. New York: Free Press.

Agar, M. (2004). We have met the other and we're all nonlinear: Ethnography as a nonlinear dynamic system. *Complexity, 10*(2), 16–22.

Albright, J., Purohit, K. D., & Walsh, C. (2006). Hybridity, globalization and literacy education in the context of New York City's Chinatown. *Pedagogies: An International Journal, 1*(4), 221–242.

Alim, H. S., Ibrahim, A., & Pennycook, A. (Eds.). (2009). *Global linguistic flows: Hip-hop cultures, youth identities and the politics of language*. London: Routledge.

Anderson, B. (1983). *Imagined communities: Reflections on the origin and spread of nationalism*. London: Verso.

Appadurai, A. (1996). *Modernity at large: Cultural dimensions of globalization*. Minneapolis: University of Minnesota Press.

Appadurai, A. (2006). *Fear of small numbers: An essay on the geography of anger*. London: Duke University Press.

Austin, H., Dwyer, B., & Freebody, P. (2003). *Schooling the child: The making of students in classrooms*. London: RoutledgeFalmer.

Baildon, M., & Damico, J. (2010). *Social studies as new literacies in global society: Relational cosmopolitanism in the classroom*. New York: Routledge.

Baker, W. D. and Green, J. (2007). Limits to certainty in interpreting video data: Interactional ethnography and disciplinary knowledge. *Pedagogies, 2*(3), 191–204.

Baker-Sperry, L., & Grauerholz, L. (2003). The pervasiveness and persistence of the feminine beauty ideal in children's fairy tales. *Gender & Society, 17*(5), 711–726.

Bakhtin, M. M. (1981). *The dialogic imagination: Four essays*. Austin, TX: University of Texas Press.

Barnard, R. (2009). Fictions of the global. *Novel: A Forum on Fiction, 42*(2), 207–215.

Bateson, G. (1955/1972). A theory of play and fantasy. In G. Bateson (Ed.), *Steps to an ecology of mind* (pp. 177–193). San Francisco, CA: Chandler.

Bauman, R., & Briggs, C. (1990). Poetics and performance as critical perspectives on language and social life. *Annual Review of Anthropology, 19*, 59–88.

Bauman, Z. (1998). *Globalization: The human consequences*. London: Polity Press.

Bauman, Z. (2007). *Consuming life*. Malden, MA: Polity Press.

Bazalgette, C. (2010). *Teaching media in primary schools*. London: Sage.

Beard, L. (2003). Whose life in the mirror?: Examining three Mexican telenovelas as cultural and commercial products. *Studies in Latin American Popular Culture, 22*(1), 73.

Black, R. (2005). Access and affiliation: The literacy and composition practices of English language learners in an online fanfiction community. *Journal of Adolescent and Adult Literacy, 49*, 118–128.

Black, R. (2009). Online fanfiction, global identities, and imagination. *Research in the Teaching of English, 43*(4), 397–425.

Blaise, M. (2005). *Playing it straight: Uncovering gender discourses in the early childhood classroom.* New York: Routledge.

Blommaert, J. (2005). *Discourse: A critical introduction.* Cambridge: Cambridge University Press.

Blommaert, J. (2008). *Grassroots literacy: Writing, identity and voice in Central Africa.* New York: Routledge.

Bourdieu, P. (1977). *Outline of a theory of practice.* Cambridge: Cambridge University Press.

Bourdieu, P. (1986). The forms of capital. In J. Richardson (Ed.), *Handbook of theory and research for the sociology of education* (pp. 241–258). New York: Greenwood.

Britzman, D. (1991). Decentering discourses in teacher education: Or, the unleashing of unpopular things. *Journal of Education, 173*(3), 60–81.

Buckingham, D. (1997). Dissin' Disney: Critical perspectives on children's media culture. *Media, Culture, & Society, 19*, 285–293.

Buckingham, D. (2003). *Media education: Literacy, learning and contemporary culture.* Cambridge, UK: Wiley-Blackwell.

Burman, E. (1994). *Deconstructing developmental psychology.* London: Routledge.

Butler, J. (1990). *Gender trouble.* New York: Routledge.

Butler, J. (2005). *Giving an account of oneself.* New York: Fordham University Press.

Campano, G. (2007). *Immigrant students and literacy: Reading, writing, and remembering.* New York: Teachers College.

Carrington, V. (2003). "I'm in a bad mood. Let's go shopping": Interactive dolls, consumer culture and a "glocalized" model of literacy. *Journal of Early Childhood Literacy, 3*(1), 83–98.

Castells, M. (1999). Grassrooting the space of flows. *Urban Geography, 20*(4), 294–302.

Connell, R. W., & Messerschmidt, J. W. (2005). Hegemonic masculinity: Rethinking the concept. *Gender & Society, 19*(6), 829–859.

Conquergood, D. (1998). Beyond the text: Toward a performative cultural politics. In S. J. Dailey (Ed.), *The future of performance studies: Visions and revisions* (pp. 25–36). Annandale, VA: National Communication Association.

Corsaro, W. A. (1985). *Friendship and peer culture in the early years.* Norwood, NJ: Ablex.

Corsaro, W. A. (2003). *We're friends right? Inside kids' culture.* Washington, DC: Joseph Henry Press.

Corsaro, W. A. & Eder, D. (1990). Children's peer cultures. *Annual Review of Sociology, 16*, 197–220.

Couldry, N. (2003). *Media rituals: A critical approach.* New York: Routledge.

Davies, B. (1993). *Shards of glass: Children reading and writing beyond gendered identities.* Sydney, Australia: Allen & Unwin.

Davies, B. (2003). *Frogs and snails and feminist tales. Preschool children and gender* (Rev. ed.). Cresskill, NJ: Hampton Press.

Davies, B., & Saltmarsh, S. (2007). Gender economies: Literacy and the gendered production of neo-liberal subjectivities. *Gender and Education, 19*(1), 1–20.

Davis, A. M. (2006). *Good girls and wicked witches: Women in Disney's feature animation.* Eastleigh, UK: John Libby.

de Certeau, M. (1984). *The practice of everyday life.* (S. Rendall, Trans.). Berkeley: University of California Press.

Diamond, E. (Ed.). (1996). *Performance and cultural politics*. New York: Routledge.

Disney Consumer Products. (2011). *Disney Princess*. Retrieved May 14, 2011 from https://www.disneyconsumerproducts.com/Home/display.jsp?contentId=dcp_home_ourfranchises_disney_princess_us&forPrint=false&language=en&preview=false&imageShow=0&pressRoom=US&translationOf=nul&region=0.

do Rozario, R. (2004). The princess and the Magic Kingdom: Beyond nostalgia, the function of the Disney Princess. *Women's Studies in Communication, 27*(1), 34–59.

Dockter, J., Haug, D., & Lewis, C. (2010). Redefining rigor: Critical engagement, digital media, and the new English/Language Arts. *Journal of Adolescent and Adult Literacy, 53*(5), 418–420.

Dolan, J. (1993). Geographies of learning: Theatre studies, performance, and the "performative." *Theatre Journal, 45*(4), 417–441.

Duncan-Andrade, J., & Morrell, E. (2007). Critical pedagogy and popular culture in an urban secondary classroom. In P. McClaren & J. Kincheloe (Eds.), *Critical pedagogy: Where are we now?* (pp.183–200). New York: Peter Lang.

Duranti, A. (1986). The audience as co-author: An introduction. *Text, 6*(3), 239–247.

Dyson, A. H. (2003). *The brothers and sisters learn to write: Popular literacies in childhood, popular culture and school cultures*. New York: Teachers College.

Dyson, A. H. (1993). From invention to social action in early childhood literacy: A reconceptualization through dialogue about difference. *Early Childhood Research Quarterly, 8*, 409–425.

Edmiston, B., & Enciso, P. (2002). Reflections and refractions of meaning: Dialogic approaches to reading with classroom drama. In J. Flood, D. Lapp, J. R. Squire & J. M. Jensen (Eds.), *Handbook of research on teaching the English language arts* (pp. 868–880). Mahwah, NJ: Lawrence Erlbaum.

Ellsworth, E. A. (2005). *Places of learning: Media, architecture, pedagogy*. New York: RoutledgeFalmer.

Enciso, P., Volz, A., Price-Dennis, D., & Durriyah, T. (2010). Story club and configurations of literary and cross-cultural insight among immigrant and non-immigrant youth. In R. T. Jimenez, V. J. Risko, M. K. Hundley, & D. W. Rowe (Eds.), *59th Yearbook of the National Reading Conference* (pp. 366–354). Chicago: National Reading Conference.

Evans, J. (2005). *Literacy moves on: Popular culture, new technologies, and critical literacy in the elementary classroom*. Portsmouth: Heinemann.

Fernie, D., Kantor, R., & Whaley, K. L. (1995). Learning from classroom ethnographies: Same places, different times. In J. A. Hatch (Ed.), *Qualitative research in early childhood settings* (pp. 156–172). Westport, CT: Praeger.

Foucault, M. (1978). *The history of sexuality: An introduction* (Vol. 1). New York: Random House.

Foucault, M. (1995). *Discipline and punish: The birth of the prison*. New York: Random House.

Franco-Steeves, R. (2011, July 8). Droguerra. *80 Grados*. Retrieved December 20, 2013 from http://www.80grados.net/droguerra/

García-Canclini, N. (1995). *Hybrid cultures*. Minneapolis: University of Minnesota Press.

García-Canclini, N. (1999). *Globalizarnos o defender la identidad. La globalización imaginada*. Buenos Aires, Argentina: Editorial Paidós.

Garoian, C. (1999). *Performing pedagogy: Toward an art of politics*. Albany: State University of New York Press.

Gee, J. P. (1996). *Social linguistics and literacies: Ideology in discourses*. London: Taylor and Francis.

Gee, J. P. (1999). *An introduction to discourse analysis: Theory and method.* London: Routledge.

Gill, R. (2007). Postfeminist media culture: Elements of a sensibility. *European Journal of Cultural Studies, 10*(2), 147–166.

Giroux, H. A. (1999). *The mouse that roared.* Oxford, UK: Rowman and Littlefield.

Giroux, H., & McClaren, P. (Eds.). (1994). *Between borders: Pedagogy and the politics of cultural studies.* New York: Routledge.

Goffman, E. (1959). *The presentation of self in everyday life.* New York: Anchor Doubleday.

Goffman, E. (1974). *Frame analysis: An essay on the organization of experience.* New York: Harper and Row.

Goudreau, J. (2012, September 17). Disney Princess tops list of the 20 best-selling entertainment products. *Forbes.* Retrieved from http://www.forbes.com/sites/jennagoudreau/2012/09/17/disney-princess-tops-list-of-the-20-best-selling-entertainment-products/

Grosz, E. (1994). *Volatile bodies: Toward a corporeal feminism.* Bloomington: Indiana University Press.

Guerra, J. (1998). *Close to home: Oral and literate practices in a transnational Mexicano community.* New York: Teachers College.

Guerra, J. (2008). Cultivating transcultural citizenship: A writing across communities model. *Language Arts, 85*(4), 296–304.

Gutiérrez, K. (2008). Developing a sociocritical literacy in the Third Space. *Reading Research Quarterly, 43*(2), 148–164.

Gutiérrez, K. (2010). From the desk of the president: The researcher's paradox. *Educational Researcher, 39*(6), 487–488. Haas, L., Bell, E., & Sells, L. (1995). *From mouse to mermaid: The politics of film, gender, and culture.* Bloomington: Indiana University Press.

Gutiérrez, K.D., & Rogoff, B. (2003). Cultural ways of learning: Individual traits or repertoires of practice. *Educational Researcher, 32*(5), 19–25.

Hall, S. (1992). Encoding/decoding. In S. Hall, D. Hobson, A. Lowe, & P. Willis (Eds.), *Culture, media and language, (pp. 128–138).* London: Hutchinson.

Hall, S. (1996). New ethnicities. In D. Morley & K. H. Chen (Eds.), *Stuart Hall: Critical dialogues in cultural studies* (pp. 441–449). London: Routledge.

Hannerz, U. (1996). *Transnational connections: Culture, people, places.* New York: Routledge.

Hannerz, U. (n.d.). *Flows, boundaries, and hybrids: Keywords in transnational anthropology.* Retrieved November 25, 2008, from http://www.transcomm.ox.ac.uk/working%20papers/hannerz.pdf.

Harris, T.I. (2011). *Power and beauty: A love story of life on the streets.* New York, N.Y.: Harper Collins.

Heathcote, D. (1984). *Collected writings on education and drama* (L. Johnson & C. O'Neill, Eds.). Evanston, IL: Northwestern University Press.

Hecht, J. (2007). Mexico TV favors light-skinned actors. Reuters.com. Retrieved August 2010 from http://www.reuters.com/article/idUSN1338069320070814.

Hilton, M. (1996). Manufacturing make-believe: Notes on the toy and media industry for children. In M. Hilton (Ed.), *Potent fictions: Children's literacy and the challenge of popular culture* (pp. 19–46). London: Routledge.

Holland, D., Lachicotte, W., Skinner, D., & Cain, C. (1998). *Identity and agency in cultural worlds.* Cambridge, MA: Harvard University Press.

Holland, D., & Leander, K. (2004). Ethnographic studies of positioning and subjectivity: An introduction. *Ethos, 32*(2), 127–139.

Hollows, J. (2000). *Feminism, femininity, and popular culture.* Manchester: Manchester University Press.

Hunter, M. (1982). *Mastery teaching.* El Segundo, CA: TIP Publications.

Hurley, D. L. (2005). Seeing White: Children of color and the Disney fairy tale princess. *Journal of Negro Education, 74*(3), 221–232.

Inda, J. X., & Rosaldo, R. (Eds.). (2008a). *The anthropology of globalization: A reader.* Malden, MA: Blackwell.

Inda, J. X., & Rosaldo, R. (2008b). Introduction: A world in motion. In J. X. Inda & R. Rosaldo (Eds.), *The anthropology of globalization: A reader* (pp. 1–34). Malden, MA: Blackwell.

Ito, M. (2007). Technologies of the childhood imagination: Yugioh, media and everyday cultural production. In J. Karaganis and N. Jeremijenko (Eds.), *Structures of participation in digital culture* (pp. 88–111). Durham, NC: Duke University Press.

Ivanič, R. (2004). Discourses of writing and learning to write. *Language and Education, 18*(3), 220–245.

Janks, H. (2009). *Literacies and power.* New York: Routledge.

Jenkins, H. (2006). *Convergence culture: Where old and new media collide.* New York: New York University Press.

Jimenez, R. T., Smith, P. H., & Teague, T. L. (2009). Transnational and community literacies for teachers. *Journal of Adolescent and Adult Literacy, 53*(1), 16–28.

Joyce, S. (2008). Telenovelas: Consumerism as empowerment. Paper presented at the annual meeting of the NCA 94th Annual Convention, San Diego, CA. Retrieved October 26, 2010, from http://www.allacademic.com/meta/p245314_index.html.

Kane, D. (2003). Distinction worldwide?: Bourdieu's theory of taste in international context. *Poetics, 31*(5–6), 403–421.

Kearney, M. (1995). The local and the global: The anthropology of globalization and transnationalism. *Annual Review of Anthropology, 24,* 547–565.

Kellner, D., & Share, J. (2005). Toward critical media literacy: Core concepts, debates, organizations, and policy. *Discourse: Studies in the Cultural Politics of Education, 26*(3), 369–386.

Kilodavis, C., & DeSimone, S. (2010). *My princess boy,* New York: Aladdin.

Kinder, M. (1991). *Playing with power in movies, television, and video games: From Muppet Babies to Teenage Mutant Ninja Turtles.* Berkeley: University of California Press.

King, C. R., Bloodsworth-Lugo, M. K., & Lugo-Lugo, C. R. (2010). Animated representations of blackness. *Journal of African American Studies, 14*(4), 395–397.

King, N. R. (1992). The impact of context on the play of young children. In S. Kessler & B. B. Swadener (Eds.), *Reconceptualizing the early childhood curriculum: Beginning the dialogue* (pp. 43–61). New York: Teachers College.

Kraidy, M. M. (1999). The local, the global and the hybrid: A native ethnography of glocalization. *Critical Studies in Mass Communication, 16,* 454–467.

Kress, G. (1997). *Before writing: Rethinking the paths to literacy.* London: Routledge.

La Pastina, A. (2003). The centrality of telenovelas in Latin America's everyday life: Past tendencies, current knowledge, and future research. *Global Media Journal, 2*(2), 1–15.

Lacroix, C. (2004). Images of animated others: The orientalization of Disney's cartoon heroines from the Little Mermaid to the Hunchback of Notre Dame. *Popular Communication, 2*(4), 213–229.

Lam, W. S. E. (2006). Culture and learning in the context of globalization: Research directions. *Review of Research in Education, 30,* 213–237.

Lam, W. S. E. (2007). Re-envisioning language, literacy, and the immigrant subject in new mediascapes. *Pedagogies: An International Journal, 1,* 171–195.

Lankshear, C., & Knobel, M. (2006). *New literacies: Everyday practices and classroom learning* (2nd ed.). New York: Open University Press.

Leander, K. (2001). "This is our freedom bus going home right now": Producing and hybridizing space-time contexts in pedagogical discourse. *Journal of Literacy Research, 33*(4), 637–679.

Leander, K. M., & Boldt, G. M. (2013). Rereading "a pedagogy of multiliteracies": Bodies, texts, and emergence. *Journal of Literacy Research, 45*(1), 22–46.

Leander, K. M., Phillips, N. C., & Taylor, K. H. (2010). The changing social spaces of learning: Mapping new mobilities. *Review of Research in Education, 34*(1), 329–394.

Lee, C. (2007). *Culture, literacy & learning: Taking bloom in the midst of the whirlwind.* New York: Teachers College.

Lee, L. (2006). *"Becoming an American princess?": The interpretations of American popular culture by young Korean girls living in the United States.* Unpublished doctoral dissertation, Indiana University, Bloomington.

Lee, L. (2009). Young American immigrant children's interpretations of popular culture: A case study of Korean girls' perspectives on royalty in Disney films. *Journal of Early Childhood Research, 7*(2), 200–215.

Lemke, J. L. (2009). Multimodal genres and transmedia traversals: Social semiotics and the political economy of the sign. *Semiotica, 173*(1), 283–297.

Lewellen, (2002). *The anthropology of globalization.* Westport, CT: Praeger.

Lewis, (2001). *Literacy practices as social acts: Power, status and cultural norms in the classroom.* New York: Lawrence Erlbaum.

Lewison, M., Leland, C., & Harste, J. C. (2008). *Creating critical classrooms: K-8 reading and writing with an edge.* Mahwah, NJ: Lawrence Erlbaum.

Lipsitz, G. (2005). Forward: Midnight's children: Youth culture in the age of globalization. In S. Maira & E. Soep (Eds.), *Youthscapes: The popular, the national, the global* (pp. vii–xiv). Philadelphia: University of Pennsylvania Press.

Luke, A. (1992). The body literate: Discourse and inscription in early literacy training. *Linguistics and Education, 4*(1), 107–129.

Luke, A. (2004). Teaching after the market: From commodity to cosmopolitan. *Teachers College Record, 106*(7), 1422–1443.

Luke, A., Iyer, R, & Doherty, C. (2010). Literacy in the context of globalization. In D. Lapp & D. Fisher (Eds.), *Handbook of research on teaching English language arts* (3rd ed.) (pp. 104–110). Mahwah, NJ: Lawrence Erlbaum.

Luke, A., & Luke, C. (2001). Adolescence lost/childhood regained: On early intervention of the techno-subject. *Journal of Early Childhood Literacy, 1*(1), 91–120.

Lull, J. (1990). *Inside family viewing.* London: Routledge.

Macedo, D., & Gounari, P. (Eds.). (2005). *The globalization of racism.* Boulder, CO: Paradigm Publishers.

Macedo, D., & Steinberg, S.R. (Eds.). (2007). *Media literacy: A reader.* New York: Peter Lang.

Mackey, M. (2003). At play on the borders of the diagectic: Story boundaries and narrative interpretation. *Journal of Literacy Research, 35*(1), 591–632.

Madrid, S. (2011). Romantic love among peers in the preschool classroom. In S. Madrid, D. Fernie, & R. Kantor (Eds.), *Educating toddlers to teachers: Learning to see and influence the school and peer cultures of classrooms* (pp. 67–84). New York: Hampton Press.

Maira, S., & Soep, E. (Eds.). (2005). *Youthscapes: The popular, the national, the global.* Philadelphia: University of Pennsylvania Press.

Marcus, G. E. (1995). Ethnography in/of the world system: The emergence of multi-sited ethnography. *Annual Review of Anthropology, 24*, 95–117.

Marcus, G. E. (1998). *Ethnography through thick and thin.* Princeton, NJ: Princeton University Press.

Marr, K. (2008, July 30). Children targets of $1.6 billion in food ads, *Washington Post.* Retrieved December 20, 2013 from http://www.washingtonpost.com/wp-dyn/content/article/2008/07/29/AR2008072902293.html

Marsh, J. (Ed.). (2005a). *Popular culture, new media, and digital literacy in early childhood.* New York: RoutledgeFalmer.

Marsh, J. (2005b). Ritual, performance, and identity construction: Young children's engagement with popular cultural and media texts. In J. Marsh (Ed.), *Popular culture, new media and digital literacy in early childhood* (pp. 28–50). New York: RoutledgeFalmer.

Marsh, J. (2006). Popular culture in the literacy curriculum: A Bourdieuan analysis. *Reading Research Quarterly, 41*(2), 160–174.

Marshall, E. (2011). Marketing American girlhood. In E. Marshall & O. Sensoy, *Rethinking popular culture and media* (pp. 129–137). Milwaukee, WI: Rethinking Schools.

Marshall, E., & Sensoy, Ö. (2009). The same old hocus-pocus: Pedagogies of gender and sexuality in Shrek 2. *Discourse: Studies in the Cultural Politics of Education, 30*(2), 151–164.

Marshall, E., & Sensoy, Ö. (Eds.). (2011). *Rethinking popular culture and media.* Milwaukee, WI: Rethinking Schools.

Mato, D. (2002). Miami in the transnationalization of the telenovela industry: On territoriality and globalization. *Journal of Latin American Cultural Studies, 11*(2), 195–212.

Mazzarella, S. R., & Pecora, N. O. (2002). Introduction. In S. R. Mazzarella & N. O. Pecora (Eds.), *Growing up girls: Popular culture and the construction of identity* (pp. 1–10). New York: Peter Lang.

Mazarella, W. (2004). Culture, globalization, mediation. *Annual Review of Anthropology, 33*, 345–367.

McClaren, P. (1995). *Critical pedagogy and predatory culture: Oppositional politics in a postmodern era.* New York: Routledge.

McRobbie, A. (2004). Notes on *What Not to Wear* and post-feminist symbolic violence. *Sociological Review, 52*(2), 97–109.

McRobbie, A. (2009). *The aftermath of feminism: Gender, culture and social change.* London: Sage.

Medina, C. L. (2001). When Jerry Springer visits your classroom: Teaching Latina literature in a contested ground. *Theory into Practice, 40*(3), 198–204.

Medina, C. L. (2004). Drama wor(l)ds: Explorations of Latina/o realistic fiction. *Language Arts, 81*(4), 272–282.

Medina, C. L. (2006a). Critical performative literacies: Intersections among identities, social imaginations and discourses. In J. V. Hoffman, D. L. Schallert, C. M. Fairbanks, J. Worthy, & B. Maloch (Eds.), *55th Yearbook of the National Reading Conference* (pp. 182–194). Chicago: National Reading Conference.

Medina, C. L. (2006b). Identity and imagination of immigrant children: Creating commonplace locations in literary interpretation. In J. Jasinski Schneider, T. P. Crumpler, & T. Rogers (Eds.), *Process drama: An educational tool for developing multiple literacies* (pp. 53–69). Mahwah, NJ: Lawrence Erlbaum.

Medina, C. L. (2010). Reading across communities in biliteracy practices: Examining translocal discourses and cultural flows in literature discussions. *Reading Research Quarterly, 45*(1), 40–60.

Medina, C. L., & Costa, M. d. R. (2010). Collaborative voices exploring culturally and socially responsive literacies. *Language Arts, 87*(4), 263–276.

Medina, C. & Costa, M del R. (2013). Latino media and critical literacy pedagogies: Children's scripting *Telenovelas* discourses. *Journal of Language and Literacy Education* 9 (1). http://jolle.coe.uga.edu

Medina, C. L. & Perry, M. (2014). Texts, affects, and relations in cultural performance: An embodied analysis of dramatic inquiry. In P. Albers, T. Holbrook,

& A. S. Flint (Eds.), *New methods in literacy research* (pp. 115–132). New York: Routledge.

Medina, C. L., & Wohlwend, K. E. (In press). *Children converging worlds at the "playshop": Critical inquiries into literacies, performance and globalization.* New York: Routledge.

Meza, T. (2006). Las telenovelas juveniles mexicanas y las adosescentas obesas. *Revista Mexicana de Ciencias Politicas y Sociales, 48*(197), 83–94.

Moll, L. (2000). Inspired by Vygotsky: Ethnographic experiments in education. In C.D. Lee & P. Smagorinsky (Eds.), *Vygotskian perspectives in literacy research* (pp. 256–258). London: Cambridge University Press.

Morley, D. (1986). *Family television*. London: Comedia.

Muller, J. (2005). *El Soldadito de Plomo [The Little Tin Soldier].* Salamanca, Spain: Loguez Ediciones.

Murphy, P. D., & Kraidy, M. M. (Eds.). (2003). *Global media studies: Ethnographic perspectives.* New York: Routledge.

Munsch, R. (1980). *The paper bag princess.* Toronto, ON, Canada: Annick.

Munsch, R. (1991). *La princesa vestida con una bolsa de papel.* Toronto, ON, Canada: Annick Press.

NCLB. (2002). No child left behind: Closing the achievement gap in America's public schools Retrieved January 8, 2004, from http://www.ed.gov/nclb/overview/welcome/closing/index.html.

O'Neill, C. (1995). *Drama worlds: A framework for process drama.* Portsmouth, NH: Heinemann.

Ong, A. (1999). *Flexible citizenship: Cultural logistics of transnationalism.* Durham, NC: Duke University Press.

Orellana, M. F. (1996). Negotiating power through language in classroom meetings. *Linguistics and Education, 8,* 335–365.

Orenstein, P. (2011). *Cinderella ate my daughter: Dispatches from the front lines of the new girlie-girl culture.* New York: Harper.

Orozco-Gomez, G. (2006). *Comunicação social e mudança tecnológica: Um cenário de múltiplos desordenamentos. Sociedade Midiatizada.* Rio de Janeiro: Mauad.

Ortiz-Negron, L. (2007). Space out of place: Consumer culture in Puerto Rico. In F. Negron- Muntaner (Ed.), *None of the above: Puerto Ricans in the global era* (pp. 39–50). New York: Palgrave Macmillan.

Paley, V. G. (1986). *Boys and girls: Superheroes in the doll corner.* Chicago: University of Chicago Press.

Palmer, G. (2004). "The new you": Class and transformation in lifestyle television. In S. Holmes & D. Jermyn (Eds.), *Understanding reality television* (pp. 173–190). London: Routledge.

Patraka, V. (1999). *Spectacular suffering: Theatre, fascism and the Holocaust.* Bloomington: University of Indiana Press.

Pennycook, A. (2007). *Global Englishes and transcultural flows.* London: Routledge.

Pennycook, A. (2010). *Language as a local practice.* London: Routledge.

Perry, M., & Medina, C. (2011). Embodiment and performance in pedagogy: The possibility of the body in curriculum. *Journal of Curriculum Studies, 27*(3), 62–75.

Perry, M., & Medina, C. L. (2011). Embodiment and performance in pedagogy research: Investigating the possibility of the body in curriculum experience. *Journal of Curriculum Theorizing, 27*(3), 62–75.

Phelan, P. (1993). *Unmarked: The politics of performance.* New York: Routledge.

Pillow, W. S. (2003). Bodies are dangerous: Using feminist genealogy as policy studies methodology. *Journal of Education Policy, 18*(2), 145–159.

Pineau, E. L. (2002). Critical performative pedagogy: Fleshing out the politics of liberatory education. In N. Stucky & C. Wimmer (Eds.), *Teaching performance studies* (pp. 41–54). Carbondale: Southern Illinois University Press.

Pineau, E. L. (2005). Teaching is performance: Reconceptualizing a problematic metaphor. In B. K. Alexander, G. L. Anderson, & B. P. Gallegos (Eds.), *Performance theories in education* (pp. 15–39). Mahwah, NJ: Lawrence Erlbaum.

Pipher, M. (1994). *Reviving Ophelia: Saving the selves of adolescent girls.* New York: Ballantine Books.

Pugh, A. J. (2009). *Longing and belonging: Parents, children, and consumer culture.* Berkeley: University of California Press.

Rantane, T. (2004). *The media and globalization.* Thousand Oaks, CA: Sage.

Roberts, M. (2007). The fashion police: Governing the self in *What Not to Wear.* In Y. Tasker & D. Negra (Eds.), *Interrogating postfeminism.* Chapel Hill, NC: Duke University Press.

Rogow, F. (2002). ABC's of media literacy: What can pre-schoolers learn? *Telemedium: The Journal of Media Literacy, 48*(2), 175–196.

Rowsell, J. (2011). Carrying my family with me: Artifacts as emic perspectives. *Qualitative Research, 11*(3), 331–336.

Ryan, C. (2010). *How do you spell family?: Literacy, heteronormativity, and young children of lesbian mothers.* Unpublished doctoral dissertation, Ohio State University, Columbus.

Sánchez, P. (2007). Urban immigrant students: How transnationalism shapes their work learning. *Urban Review, 39*(5), 489–517.

Sanford, K. (2005). Gendered literacy experiences: The effects of expectation and opportunity for boys' and girls' learning. *Journal of Adolescent & Adult Literacy, 49*(4), 302–315.

Santos, B. de S. (2006). Globalizations. *Theory, Culture and Society, 23*(2–3), 393–399.

Santos, B. de S. (2007). Beyond abyssal thinking: From global lines to ecologies of knowledge. *Review, 30*(1), 45–89.

Sawyer, R. K. (2003). Levels of analysis in pretend play discourse: Metacommunication in conversational routines. In D. E. Lytle (Ed.), *Play and educational theory and practice* (pp. 137–157). Westport, CT: Praeger.

Scollon, R. (2001). *Mediated discourse: The nexus of practice.* London: Routledge.

Scollon, R., & Scollon, S. W. (2003). *Discourses in place.* New York: Routledge.

Scollon, R., & Scollon, S. W. (2004). *Nexus analysis: Discourse and the emerging internet.* New York: Routledge.

Scollon, R., & Scollon, S. W. (2007). Nexus analysis: Refocusing ethnography on action. *Journal of Sociolinguistics, 11*(5), 608–625.

Scollon, S. W. (2002). Nexus analysis: Expanding the circumference of discourse analysis. Paper presented at the Xerox Palo Alto Research Center Forum, Palo Alto, CA, December 12. Retrieved December 20, 2013 from http://www.parc.com/event/79/nexus-analysis.html.

Seiter, E. (1993). *Sold separately: Children and parents in consumer culture.* Piscataway, NJ: Rutgers University Press.

Siegel, M. (2006). Rereading the signs: Multimodal transformations in the field of literacy research. *Language Arts, 84*(1), 65–77.

Soep, E. (2005). Making hard-core masculinity: Teenage boys playing house. In S. Maira & E. Soep (Eds.), *Youthscapes: The popular, the national, the global* (pp.173–191). Philadelphia: University of Pennsylvania Press.

Somerville, M. (2004). Tracing bodylines: The body in feminist poststructural research. *International Journal of Qualitative Studies in Education, 17*(1), 47–63.

St. Pierre, E. A., & Pillow, W. S. (2000). *Working the ruins: Feminist poststructural theory and methods in education.* London: Routledge.

Street, B. V. (1995). *Social literacies: Critical approaches to literary development.* Singapore: Pearson Education Asia.

Street, B. V. (2003). What's "new" in New Literacy Studies?: Critical approaches to literacy in theory and practice. *Current Issues in Comparative Education, 5*(2), 77–91.

Strelitz, L. (2003). Where the global meets the local: South African youth and their experiences with local media. In P. D. Murphy & M.M. Kraidy (Eds.), *Global media studies: Ethnographic perspectives* (pp. 234–256). New York: Routledge.

Sun, C. F. (2011). Mulan's mixed messages: Disney's film drags Chinese civilization through the mud. In E. Marshall & Ö. Sensoy (Eds.), *Rethinking popular culture and media* (pp. 106–109). Milwaukee, WI: Rethinking Schools.

Titley, G. (2003). Cultivating habitats of meaning-broadcasting, participation and interculturalism. *Irish Communications Review, 9*(5), 1–11. Retrieved December 20, 2013 from http://www.icr.dit.ie/volume9/articles/Titley.pdf

Tobin, J. (2000). *"Good guys don't wear hats": Children's talk about media.* New York: Teachers College.

Tobin, J. (Ed.). (2004). *Pikachu's global adventure: The rise and fall of Pokémon.* Durham, NC: Duke University Press.

Vasquez, V. (2004). *Negotiating critical literacies with young children.* Mahwah, NJ: Lawrence Erlbaum.

Vasquez, V. (In press). *Negotiating critical literacies with young children* (2nd ed.). Mahwah, NJ: Lawrence Erlbaum.

Vasquez, V. M., & Felderman, C. B. (2012). *Technology and critical literacy in early childhood.* New York: Routledge.

Walkerdine, V. (1984). Some day my prince will come. In A. McRobbie & M. Nava (Eds.), *Gender and generation* (pp.162–184). London: Macmillan.

Walkerdine, V. (1999). Violent boys and precocious girls: Regulating childhood at the end of the millennium. *Contemporary Issues in Early Childhood, 1*(1), 3–23.

Weltsek, G., & Medina, C. (2007). In search of the glocal through process drama. In M. V. Blackburn & C. Clark (Eds.), *Literacy research for political action and social change* (pp. 255–275). New York: Peter Lang.

Werner, J. F. (2006). How women are using television to domesticate globalization: A case study on the reception and consumption of telenovelas in Senegal. *Visual Anthropology, 19*, 443–472.

Whannel, G. (2001). *Media sports stars: Masculinities and moralities.* London: Routledge.

What Not to Wear. (2009). Retrieved September 30, 2011, from http://tlc.howstuffworks.com/tv/what- not-to-wear.

Whitmore, K. F., & Crowell, C. G. (1994). *Inventing a classroom: Life in a bilingual whole language learning community.* York, ME: Stenhouse.

Wilk, R. R. (2000). A critique of desire: Distaste and dislike in consumer behavior. *Consumption, Markets and Culture, 1*(2), 97–196.

Wohlwend, K. E. (2005). Chasing friendship: Acceptance, rejection, and recess play. *Childhood Education, 81*(2), 77–82.

Wohlwend, K. E. (2007). Friendship meeting or blocking circle? Identities in the laminated spaces of a playground conflict. *Contemporary Issues in Early Childhood, 8*(1), 73–88.

Wohlwend, K. E. (2008). Play as a literacy of possibilities: Expanding meanings in practices, materials, and spaces. *Language Arts, 86*(2), 127–136.

Wohlwend, K. E. (2009a). Damsels in discourse: Girls consuming and producing gendered identity texts through Disney Princess Play. *Reading Research Quarterly, 44*(1), 57–83.

Wohlwend, K. E. (2009b). Dilemmas and discourses of learning to write: Assessment as a contested site. *Language Arts, 86*(5), 341–351.

Wohlwend, K. E. (2009c). Mapping multimodal literacy practices through mediated discourse analysis: Identity revision in *What Not to Wear.* In K. M. Leander, D. W. Rowe, R. Jimenez, D. Compton, D. K. Dickinson, Y. Kim, & V. Risko (Eds.), *Fifty-eighth Yearbook of the National Reading Conference* (pp. 66–81). San Antonio, TX: National Reading Conference.

Wohlwend, K. E. (2011). *Playing their way into literacies: Reading, writing, and belonging in the early childhood classroom.* New York: Teachers College.

Wohlwend, K. E. (2012). The boys who would be princesses: Playing with gender identity intertexts in Disney Princess transmedia. *Gender and Education, 24*(6), 593–610.

Wohlwend, K. E. (In press). Playing to belong: Sharing princesses and mediating preschool cultures. In R. Haines & M. Forman-Brunell (Eds.), *Princess cultures: Mediating girls' imaginations and identities.* New York: Peter Lang.

Wohlwend, K. E., Buchholz, B. A., Wessel-Powell, C., Coggin, L. S., & Husbye, N. E. (2013). *Literacy playshop: Playing with new literacies and popular media in the early childhood classroom.* New York: Teachers College.

Wohlwend, K. E., & Lewis, C. (2010). Critical literacy, critical engagement, and digital technology: Convergence and embodiment in glocal spheres. In D. Lapp & D. Fisher (Eds.), *Handbook of research on teaching English language arts* (3rd ed.) (pp. 188–194). New York: Routledge.

Wohlwend, K. E., & Medina, C. L. (2012). Media as nexus of practice: Remaking identities in *What Not to Wear. Discourse: Studies in the Cultural Politics of Education, 33*(4), 545–560.

Wohlwend, K. E., & Medina, C. L. (2013). Producing cultural imaginaries in the playshop. In K. F. Whitmore & R. J. Meyer (Eds.), *Reclaiming writing: Composing spaces for identities, relationships, and actions* (pp. 198–209). New York: Routledge.

Woodward, S. (2007). *Why women wear what they wear.* Oxford: Berg.

Index

Note: Page numbers ending in "f" refer to figures. Page numbers ending in "t" refer to tables.